Mastering Small Business Success

Strategies and Insights

Nolan Davis

Mastering Small Business Success

Strategies and Insights

Published by
Nolan Davis

ISBN
9798335975902

Copyright Notice

The content of this book is protected by copyright law. It is intended for personal use only. Unauthorized reproduction, distribution, modification, sale, use, quoting, or paraphrasing of any part or all of the content of this book without the author's or publisher's consent is prohibited.

All rights for translation, adaptation, and reproduction by any means are reserved worldwide. According to the Copyright Act, any copying or reproduction strictly for private use and not for collective use is permitted. However, any total or partial representation or reproduction without the author's or rights holder's consent is illegal and constitutes copyright infringement, subject to legal penalties.

Disclaimer:

By reading this document, the reader agrees that the author is not liable for any direct or indirect losses resulting from the use of the information contained in this document, including but not limited to errors, omissions, or inaccuracies.

Copyright © Nolan Davis – All rights reserved

TABLE OF CONTENTS

Introduction 4
    The Importance of Small Business Success.............. 5
    Setting the Stage for Success................................... 11
1. The Foundations of Small Business Success............... 19
    1.1. Understanding Your Market............................ 20
    1.2. Building a Strong Brand.................................. 28
2. Effective Marketing Strategies..................................... 39
    2.1. Digital Marketing Essentials........................... 40
    2.2. Traditional Marketing Techniques.................. 51
3. Financial Management for Small Businesses........ 62
    3.1. Budgeting and Forecasting............................. 63
    3.2. Managing Cash Flow...................................... 72
4. Leadership and Team Building..................................... 83
    4.1. Effective Leadership Traits............................. 84
    4.2. Building a High-Performing Team.................... 92
5. Scaling and Expansion.. 105
    5.1. Preparing for Growth..................................... 106
    5.2. Entering New Markets................................... 116
Conclusion... 127
    Reflecting on the Journey..................................... 128
    Final Thoughts and Encouragement..................... 137
A Personal Message and Acknowledgements........ 148

INTRODUCTION

Welcome to "Mastering Small Business Success: Strategies and Insights." Whether you're a seasoned entrepreneur or just starting your journey, this book is crafted to guide you through the intricate landscape of small business management. Think of it as a roadmap designed to lead you from where you are now to the thriving business you envision.

Imagine being on a cross-country road trip. At the start, the path may seem daunting, filled with unknowns and potential detours. But with a well-planned route, a reliable vehicle, and a sense of adventure, the journey transforms into an exciting exploration of new opportunities. This book serves as your GPS, offering clear directions, practical advice, and inspiring stories to keep you motivated along the way.

From my early days, helping out at my parents' small bakery in Austin, Texas, I learned firsthand the challenges and rewards of running a business. Those experiences, combined with my professional journey, have equipped me with insights that I'm eager to share with you. Each chapter in this book is a pit stop, where you'll gather valuable tools and strategies to help you navigate the complexities of entrepreneurship.

By the end of this journey, you'll have a comprehensive understanding of how to build and grow a successful small business. So, buckle up, stay open to learning, and let's embark on this transformative adventure together.

THE IMPORTANCE OF SMALL BUSINESS SUCCESS

THE BACKBONE OF THE ECONOMY

Small businesses are the backbone of the American economy. They embody the entrepreneurial spirit that has driven innovation and economic growth in the United States for centuries. Imagine the bustling main streets of small towns, each storefront representing the hard work, dreams, and resilience of its owners. These businesses create jobs, foster community, and drive local economies, making them vital to the nation's overall economic health.

Let's take a closer look at why small businesses are so crucial. According to the U.S. Small Business Administration, small businesses make up 99.9% of all U.S. businesses. They employ nearly half of the private workforce and are responsible for creating two out of every three new jobs. This sheer scale highlights their significant role in driving employment and innovation. For example, companies like Apple and Amazon, which started in garages, have grown to become global powerhouses, showing the potential of small businesses to make a massive impact.

Furthermore, small businesses contribute to the diversity and resilience of the economy. They often cater to niche markets and bring unique products and services to the table, fostering innovation and competition. This diversity ensures that the economy is not overly dependent on a few large corporations. During economic downturns, small businesses can adapt more quickly than larger firms, finding creative solutions to stay afloat and even thrive. This agility was evident during the COVID-19 pandemic, where many small businesses pivoted their models to meet changing consumer needs, whether through online sales, delivery services, or new product lines.

Consider the story of Jane, who owns a small bookstore in Seattle. Faced with declining foot traffic during the pandemic, Jane quickly adapted by enhancing her online presence, offering virtual book readings, and creating a local delivery service. Her ability to pivot not only saved her business but also kept her community engaged and supported. Stories like Jane's highlight the ingenuity and resilience that small businesses bring to the economy.

Moreover, small businesses often drive community development. They sponsor local events, support schools and charities, and create a sense of place and identity for communities. They are the coffee shops where friends meet, the bakeries that provide your favorite treats, and the boutiques that offer unique finds. These businesses help foster strong, vibrant communities where people want to live and work. The relationship is symbiotic: thriving communities support local businesses, and successful businesses, in turn, reinvest in their communities.

Take, for example, the annual farmers market in a small town. This event not only provides local farmers and artisans a platform to sell their goods but also brings the community together, fostering a sense of belonging and mutual support. The success of these markets can often spill over into other local businesses, creating a vibrant local economy.

The importance of small businesses also extends to fostering innovation and entrepreneurship. Small businesses are often the first to bring new ideas and products to market. Their size allows them to be nimble and take risks that larger companies might avoid. This spirit of innovation is crucial for economic growth and competitiveness. Entrepreneurs like Sara Blakely, who founded Spanx with a single product idea, demonstrate how small businesses can revolutionize industries and create new market segments.

Small businesses also play a critical role in addressing societal issues. They often lead the way in adopting sustainable practices, supporting local supply chains, and championing social causes. By aligning their business goals with social and environmental objectives, they create a positive impact that goes beyond profit. For instance, Tom's Shoes started with a simple idea: for every pair of shoes sold, they would donate a pair to a child in need. This model not only built a successful business but also made a significant social impact.

In conclusion, small businesses are much more than economic entities; they are vital to the fabric of our society. They drive job creation, foster innovation, support communities, and contribute to the overall economic resilience. Understanding their importance is the first step in appreciating the strategies and insights that will be discussed throughout this book. As we delve deeper, you'll see how your small business can not only succeed but also contribute to the larger economic and social ecosystem.

CHALLENGES AND OPPORTUNITIES

Running a small business is a journey filled with both challenges and opportunities. Understanding these elements is crucial for navigating the path to success. Let's delve into some of the common challenges small businesses face and the opportunities that arise from overcoming them.

One of the most significant challenges small businesses encounter is financial management. Unlike large corporations, small businesses often operate with limited capital and tighter margins. This constraint requires careful budgeting, effective cash flow management, and strategic investment. For many entrepreneurs, managing finances can feel like walking a tightrope, where one misstep could lead to severe consequences.

Take the example of Sarah, who runs a small artisanal bakery in Brooklyn. In her early days, managing cash flow was a constant struggle. Seasonal fluctuations in sales and unexpected expenses often left her in a tight spot. However, by adopting stringent financial practices, like maintaining an emergency fund and closely monitoring her cash flow, Sarah was able to stabilize her finances and invest in expanding her product line, ultimately growing her business.

Another common challenge is competition. Small businesses often compete against larger, more established companies with greater resources. This competition can be daunting, but it also presents an opportunity to differentiate and carve out a niche market. Small businesses can leverage their agility and personal touch to offer unique products and exceptional customer service that larger companies may struggle to match.

Consider the story of Mike, who owns a small coffee shop in Portland. Surrounded by big-name coffee chains, Mike faced stiff competition. Instead of trying to compete on price, he focused on creating a unique customer experience. By offering locally sourced pastries, hosting community events, and remembering regular customers by name, Mike built a loyal customer base that values the personal touch his coffee shop provides.

Marketing is another area where small businesses face challenges. With limited budgets, reaching potential customers and building brand awareness can be difficult. However, the rise of digital marketing has leveled the playing field, offering cost-effective ways to connect with a broader audience. Social media platforms, email marketing, and content creation allow small businesses to engage with customers directly and build strong online communities.

For example, Jenny, who runs a handmade jewelry business, used social media to her advantage. By creating engaging content, collaborating with influencers, and running targeted ads, she was able to reach customers far beyond her local area. Her online presence not only drove sales but also built a loyal following who eagerly awaited her new collections.

Human resources management is another critical challenge. Small businesses often operate with smaller teams, making each employee's contribution vital. Attracting and retaining talent can be challenging, especially when competing with larger companies that offer higher salaries and more extensive benefits. However, small businesses can create a positive and motivating work environment by offering flexible working hours, opportunities for growth, and a close-knit company culture.

Think of David, who runs a tech startup. By fostering a culture of innovation, offering professional development opportunities, and ensuring a healthy work-life balance, he was able to attract talented individuals passionate about his vision. This dedicated team became the backbone of his business, driving it to new heights.

Despite these challenges, small businesses also have unique opportunities that can drive their success. The close connection with their customers allows them to gather direct feedback and adapt quickly to changing needs and preferences. This responsiveness can lead to higher customer satisfaction and loyalty.

Moreover, small businesses often play a vital role in their local communities, which can be leveraged to build strong community ties and local support. Sponsoring local events, collaborating with other small businesses, and participating in community initiatives can enhance a business's reputation and customer base.

Lastly, small businesses have the opportunity to innovate and disrupt markets. Their size allows them to experiment with new ideas and pivot quickly based on market feedback. This agility is a significant advantage in a rapidly changing business environment.

In conclusion, while small businesses face numerous challenges, these hurdles also present opportunities for growth and differentiation. By effectively managing finances, leveraging digital marketing, fostering a positive work environment, and staying connected with their communities, small businesses can turn challenges into stepping stones for success. The journey may be tough, but with resilience and strategic planning, the rewards can be substantial.

Setting the Stage for Success

Defining Your Vision and Mission

Defining your vision and mission is the cornerstone of any successful small business. These statements act as your guiding star, providing direction and purpose for your business decisions and actions. Let's explore how to craft meaningful vision and mission statements and why they are vital for your business's success.

Vision Statement: The Dream

Your vision statement encapsulates the long-term aspirations of your business. It is a forward-looking declaration of what you aim to achieve in the future. Think of it as the dream you are working towards, the ultimate impact you want your business to have on the world.

When crafting your vision statement, it's important to think big and be aspirational. Reflect on what you truly want to accomplish and how you want your business to be perceived in the long run. For example, let's say you run a small organic skincare company. Your vision might be: "To become the leading provider of sustainable skincare products that enhance natural beauty and promote environmental health."

This vision is bold and inspiring. It communicates a clear long-term goal and sets the stage for strategic planning and decision-making. It's not just about being the best in the market; it's about making a positive impact on your customers and the planet.

Mission Statement: The Path

While the vision statement focuses on the future, the mission statement is about the present. It defines the purpose of your business and the approach you will take to achieve your vision. Your mission statement should clearly articulate what your business does, who it serves, and how it delivers value.

Let's continue with the organic skincare company example. A strong mission statement might be: "To create high-quality, eco-friendly skincare products that enhance natural beauty using sustainably sourced ingredients, while educating and empowering our customers to make environmentally conscious choices."

This mission statement is concise yet comprehensive. It outlines the company's commitment to quality, sustainability, and customer education. It serves as a practical guide for daily operations and helps align the team with the company's core values.

Creating Your Vision and Mission Statements

Creating vision and mission statements requires introspection and clarity. Here are some steps to help you define these critical components:

1. **Reflect on Your Values and Purpose:**
    - Consider what motivates you to run your business. What are your core values and

beliefs? What impact do you want to have on your customers and the community?

2. **Identify Your Unique Strengths:**
   - Think about what sets your business apart from the competition. What unique strengths and capabilities do you bring to the table? How do these align with your long-term goals?
3. **Engage Your Team:**
   - If you have a team, involve them in the process. Their perspectives can provide valuable insights and help create a sense of shared purpose. Hold brainstorming sessions to gather ideas and feedback.
4. **Draft and Refine:**
   - Start by drafting initial versions of your vision and mission statements. Don't worry about getting it perfect on the first try. Refine the statements through multiple iterations, seeking input from trusted advisors and team members.
5. **Ensure Clarity and Conciseness:**
   - Your statements should be clear and concise, avoiding jargon and complex language. They should be easy to understand and remember, serving as effective communication tools both internally and externally.

Living Your Vision and Mission

Once you've defined your vision and mission statements, the next step is to integrate them into every aspect of your business. Here's how:

1. **Communicate Consistently:**
   - Display your vision and mission statements prominently in your workplace and on your website. Ensure that all marketing materials, social media content, and customer communications reflect these core messages.
2. **Align Business Decisions:**
   - Use your vision and mission as a framework for decision-making. Whether you're considering a new product line, marketing strategy, or partnership, ask yourself if it aligns with your vision and mission.
3. **Engage Your Team:**
   - Make sure your team understands and embraces the vision and mission. Regularly discuss how their work contributes to the larger goals and recognize their efforts in helping achieve them.
4. **Evaluate and Adjust:**
   - Periodically review your vision and mission statements to ensure they remain relevant and inspiring. As your business evolves, be open to making adjustments that reflect new goals and insights.

Defining your vision and mission is not just a one-time exercise; it's an ongoing process that evolves with your business. These statements are powerful tools that can inspire, guide, and align your team and customers toward a shared purpose. By setting a clear vision and mission, you lay the foundation for sustainable success and meaningful impact.

Creating a Strategic Plan

Creating a strategic plan is akin to mapping out the route for your business journey. It's a comprehensive blueprint that outlines your goals, strategies, and actions required to achieve your vision and mission. Let's explore the essential components of a strategic plan and how to craft one that drives your small business toward success.

1. Define Your Goals:

The first step in creating a strategic plan is to set clear, measurable goals. These goals should align with your vision and mission, providing specific targets to strive for. Think of your goals as the destinations on your roadmap, giving direction and purpose to your efforts.

When defining your goals, use the SMART criteria:

- **Specific:** Clearly define what you want to achieve.
- **Measurable:** Ensure that you can track progress and measure outcomes.
- **Achievable:** Set realistic goals that are attainable given your resources.
- **Relevant:** Align your goals with your overall business objectives.
- **Time-bound:** Set deadlines to create a sense of urgency and focus.

For instance, if you run a small bakery, a SMART goal could be: "Increase online sales by 20% over the next six months by launching a new e-commerce platform and digital marketing campaign."

2. Conduct a SWOT Analysis:

A SWOT analysis helps you understand your business's internal strengths and weaknesses, as well as external opportunities and threats. This analysis provides valuable insights that can inform your strategic decisions and help you capitalize on strengths while addressing weaknesses.

- **Strengths:** Identify what your business does well. What are your unique selling points? What resources and capabilities give you an advantage?
- **Weaknesses:** Recognize areas where your business could improve. What limitations or challenges do you face?
- **Opportunities:** Look for external factors that could benefit your business. Are there market trends or gaps you can exploit?
- **Threats:** Consider external factors that could pose risks. Are there competitors, economic shifts, or regulatory changes that could impact your business?

For example, a SWOT analysis for a local coffee shop might reveal strengths like a loyal customer base and high-quality products, weaknesses such as limited seating, opportunities like increasing demand for online orders, and threats like the opening of a new coffee chain nearby.

3. Develop Strategies:

With your goals and SWOT analysis in hand, the next step is to develop strategies to achieve your objectives. Strategies are the broad approaches you will take to reach your goals. They provide a high-level framework for your action plans.

Consider the bakery example. If the goal is to increase online sales, the strategies might include:

- Enhancing the user experience on your e-commerce site.
- Implementing targeted digital marketing campaigns.
- Expanding your product range to include items that are easy to ship.
- Partnering with local delivery services to offer same-day delivery.

4. Create Action Plans:

Strategies provide direction, but action plans break down these strategies into specific, actionable steps. Each action plan should detail what needs to be done, who is responsible, the resources required, and the timeline for completion.

For instance, an action plan to enhance the e-commerce site might include:

- **Action:** Redesign website layout.
    - **Responsible:** Web designer.
    - **Resources:** Budget for design and development.
    - **Timeline:** Complete by end of Month 1.
- **Action:** Add customer reviews and ratings.
    - **Responsible:** Marketing team.
    - **Resources:** Time to collect and integrate reviews.
    - **Timeline:** Complete by end of Month 2.
- **Action:** Optimize site for mobile devices.
    - **Responsible:** IT team.
    - **Resources:** Mobile optimization tools.
    - **Timeline:** Complete by end of Month 3.

5. Monitor and Adjust:

A strategic plan is not static; it requires regular monitoring and adjustments. Track your progress against your goals and make data-driven decisions to stay on course. Use key performance indicators (KPIs) to measure success and identify areas needing improvement.

For example, if online sales are not increasing as expected, review your digital marketing efforts. Are you targeting the right audience? Is your website conversion rate satisfactory? Adjust your strategies and action plans based on your findings to ensure continuous improvement.

6. Engage Your Team:

Ensure that your entire team understands and is committed to the strategic plan. Regularly communicate progress, celebrate milestones, and encourage feedback. A motivated and informed team is essential for executing the plan effectively.

Conclusion:

Creating a strategic plan is a dynamic and ongoing process that requires clear goals, thorough analysis, well-defined strategies, actionable steps, and continuous monitoring. By following these steps, you can chart a course for your small business that navigates challenges, leverages opportunities, and drives sustainable success. Remember, a well-crafted strategic plan is your roadmap to achieving your business vision and mission.

Chapter 1

1. The Foundations of Small Business Success

Embarking on the journey of small business ownership is both exhilarating and challenging. The foundation you lay at the beginning will determine the strength and resilience of your business as it grows. In this chapter, we will explore the essential elements that form the bedrock of a successful small business.

Think of your business as a house. Before you can start building the walls and adding the finishing touches, you need a solid foundation. This foundation includes understanding your market, defining your brand, and establishing strong operational practices. Without these critical components, even the most innovative business ideas can falter.

As we delve into the foundational aspects of small business success, we will cover market research techniques to help you understand your target audience and identify opportunities. We will discuss the importance of building a strong brand that resonates with customers and sets you apart from competitors. Additionally, we will explore the operational practices that streamline processes and enhance efficiency, ensuring your business runs smoothly from day one.

In this chapter, you will find practical advice, real-life examples, and actionable steps to lay a robust foundation for your business. By taking the time to establish these key elements, you will be better equipped to navigate challenges, seize opportunities, and build a business that not only survives but thrives in the competitive marketplace.

Get ready to dig deep and lay the groundwork for your entrepreneurial success. Let's start building the solid foundation your business needs to stand the test of time.

1.1. Understanding Your Market

1.1.1. Market Research Techniques

Understanding your market is a crucial step in building a successful small business. Market research allows you to gather valuable insights about your target audience, competitors, and industry trends. These insights enable you to make informed decisions and tailor your products or services to meet customer needs effectively.

Why Market Research Matters

Market research is like a compass that guides your business strategy. It helps you identify who your customers are, what they want, and how you can serve them better than your competitors. Without it, you're navigating your business decisions in the dark, relying on assumptions rather than facts.

Types of Market Research

There are two main types of market research: primary and secondary. Each provides unique insights and can be used to complement each other.

1. **Primary Research:**
   - Primary research involves gathering new data directly from potential customers. This can be done through surveys, interviews, focus groups, and observations. The advantage of primary research is that it provides specific, up-to-date information directly related to your business.
   - For example, if you're planning to open a new coffee shop, conducting surveys in your local area can help you understand customer preferences for coffee flavors, pricing, and additional services like Wi-Fi or seating arrangements.
2. **Secondary Research:**
   - Secondary research involves analyzing existing data collected by others. This can include industry reports, competitor analysis, and statistical data from government agencies. Secondary research is useful for gaining a broader understanding of market trends and benchmarking your business against competitors.
   - Continuing with the coffee shop example, you might analyze industry reports on coffee consumption trends, demographics of coffee drinkers, and successful business models in the coffee industry.

Conducting Effective Market Research

Here are some practical steps to conduct effective market research for your small business:

1. **Define Your Objectives:**
   - Start by clearly defining what you want to achieve with your market research. Are you looking to understand customer preferences, identify market gaps, or analyze competitor strengths and weaknesses? Clear objectives will guide your research process and ensure you collect relevant data.
2. **Identify Your Target Audience:**
   - Knowing who your customers are is fundamental. Create detailed customer profiles based on demographics (age, gender, income, etc.), psychographics (lifestyle, values, interests), and behaviors (buying habits, product usage). This helps you tailor your research efforts to gather insights from the right people.
3. **Choose Your Research Methods:**
   - Select the most appropriate research methods based on your objectives and target audience. For primary research, consider online surveys for a broad reach, face-to-face interviews for in-depth insights, or focus groups for interactive discussions. For secondary research, utilize industry reports, online databases, and competitor websites.
4. **Collect Data:**
   - Execute your research plan by collecting data from your chosen sources. Ensure you gather a sufficient sample size to make your findings statistically significant and representative of your target audience. Use

tools like SurveyMonkey for online surveys, or social media platforms to engage with potential customers.
5. **Analyze the Data:**
    - Once you've collected the data, analyze it to identify patterns, trends, and actionable insights. Use statistical tools and software like Excel, SPSS, or Tableau to process and visualize the data. Look for correlations and anomalies that can inform your business decisions.
6. **Interpret and Apply Insights:**
    - Translate your research findings into actionable strategies. For example, if your survey reveals that customers prefer eco-friendly packaging, consider incorporating sustainable materials into your product packaging. If competitor analysis shows a gap in the market for a specific service, explore the feasibility of offering that service.

Real-Life Example:

Let's take the example of Emily, who wanted to start a boutique fitness studio in her neighborhood. She conducted primary research by distributing online surveys and hosting focus groups with local residents to understand their fitness preferences, pricing expectations, and preferred class timings. She complemented this with secondary research, analyzing fitness industry trends and local competitor offerings.

Emily's research revealed a high demand for early morning yoga classes and a lack of fitness options for working parents. Armed with this information, she tailored her business plan to offer early morning yoga sessions and childcare services during workout times. Her market research not only helped her design a compelling value proposition but also gave her the confidence to launch her studio with a clear understanding of her target market.

Conclusion:

Market research is an indispensable tool for small business success. By understanding your market, you can make informed decisions that align with customer needs, differentiate your business from competitors, and seize market opportunities. Investing time and resources in thorough market research will pay off by providing a solid foundation for your business strategy and growth.

1.1.2. IDENTIFYING YOUR TARGET AUDIENCE

Identifying your target audience is a fundamental step in building a successful small business. Knowing who your customers are enables you to tailor your products, services, and marketing efforts to meet their specific needs and preferences. This section will guide you through the process of defining and understanding your target audience, helping you create a focused and effective business strategy.

Why Identifying Your Target Audience Matters

Understanding your target audience is crucial because it allows you to:

- Develop products and services that meet their specific needs.
- Craft marketing messages that resonate and engage.
- Allocate resources efficiently by focusing on the most promising customer segments.
- Build stronger customer relationships and loyalty.

Without a clear understanding of your target audience, your business efforts can become scattered and less effective, leading to wasted resources and missed opportunities.

Steps to Identify Your Target Audience

1. **Analyze Your Existing Customers:**
    - Start by looking at your current customer base. Who are they? What do they buy? Why do they choose your products or services over competitors? Use customer data, feedback, and sales records to identify common characteristics and behaviors.
2. **Segment Your Market:**
    - Market segmentation involves dividing your broader market into smaller, more defined groups based on shared characteristics. Common segmentation criteria include:
        - **Demographic:** Age, gender, income, education, occupation.
        - **Geographic:** Location, climate, population density.
        - **Psychographic:** Lifestyle, values, interests, attitudes.

- **Behavioral:** Buying habits, product usage, brand loyalty.
  - For example, if you run a specialty coffee shop, you might segment your market into young professionals who prefer specialty brews, students looking for study spaces, and retirees seeking a social environment.
3. **Create Customer Personas:**
   - Customer personas are detailed profiles of your ideal customers. They bring your target audience to life by combining demographic, psychographic, and behavioral information. Personas help you understand your customers on a deeper level and tailor your marketing efforts accordingly.
   - To create a customer persona, gather data from various sources such as surveys, interviews, and social media analytics. Then, develop a fictional but realistic representation of your ideal customer. Include details like their name, age, occupation, hobbies, challenges, and buying motivations.
   - For instance, one of your personas for the coffee shop might be "Tech-Savvy Taylor," a 28-year-old software developer who loves trying new coffee flavors and values sustainability. Taylor prefers cafes with fast Wi-Fi and a cozy atmosphere for remote work.
4. **Understand Customer Pain Points and Needs:**
   - Identify the problems and challenges your target audience faces that your product or

service can solve. Understanding these pain points allows you to position your offerings as the ideal solution.
- For example, if your target audience consists of busy parents, their pain points might include finding convenient meal options and balancing family time. A meal delivery service could cater to these needs by offering healthy, ready-to-eat meals that save time and reduce stress.

5. **Research Competitors:**
   - Analyze your competitors to understand who they are targeting and how they are positioning their products or services. Identify gaps in the market that your business can fill. Look for opportunities to differentiate your offerings based on the unmet needs of your target audience.

6. **Utilize Data and Analytics:**
   - Leverage data and analytics tools to gain deeper insights into your target audience. Use Google Analytics to track website traffic and user behavior, social media analytics to understand engagement patterns, and customer relationship management (CRM) systems to analyze sales and customer interactions.

7. **Engage with Your Audience:**
   - Directly engaging with your audience through surveys, interviews, focus groups, and social media interactions provides valuable qualitative insights. Ask open-ended questions to uncover their

motivations, preferences, and opinions about your products or services.

Real-Life Example:

Let's look at John, who owns a boutique fitness studio. Initially, John marketed his services to a broad audience, but he noticed that his classes were mostly attended by young professionals and busy parents. To better understand these groups, he conducted surveys and created two customer personas: "Fitness-Focused Fiona," a 32-year-old marketing executive who values high-intensity workouts and "Parent-on-the-Go Paul," a 40-year-old father of two looking for flexible class schedules.

By focusing his marketing efforts on these personas, John tailored his messaging, offering early morning and late evening classes for Fiona and weekend family-friendly sessions for Paul. He also emphasized the studio's convenient location and high-quality instructors, addressing the specific needs and preferences of his target audience.

Conclusion:

Identifying your target audience is a continuous process that evolves as your business grows. By understanding who your customers are, what they need, and how they behave, you can create a more effective business strategy that resonates with your audience and drives success. Remember, the more you know about your customers, the better you can serve them, and the stronger your business will become.

1.2. BUILDING A STRONG BRAND

1.2.1. Brand Identity and Positioning

Building a strong brand is essential for differentiating your business in a crowded marketplace and creating a lasting connection with your customers. Your brand identity and positioning communicate who you are, what you stand for, and why customers should choose you over competitors. Let's explore how to develop a compelling brand identity and position your brand effectively.

Brand Identity: Crafting Your Business's Persona

Your brand identity is the visual and emotional representation of your business. It includes your logo, colors, typography, tone of voice, and overall style. Creating a cohesive and memorable brand identity involves several key elements:

1. **Logo:**
   - Your logo is the visual cornerstone of your brand. It should be simple, memorable, and reflective of your business values and mission. Think of iconic logos like Apple's apple or Nike's swoosh—each is instantly recognizable and conveys the essence of the brand.
2. **Color Palette:**
   - Colors evoke emotions and associations. Choose a color palette that aligns with your brand's personality and appeals to your target audience. For example, blue often conveys trust and professionalism, while green can represent health and sustainability. Consistency in color usage

across all marketing materials helps reinforce brand recognition.
3. **Typography:**
    - Fonts play a crucial role in brand perception. Select fonts that are easy to read and reflect your brand's tone. A modern, sleek font can convey innovation, while a classic serif font might suggest tradition and reliability.
4. **Visual Elements:**
    - Beyond your logo and colors, consider other visual elements such as patterns, icons, and imagery that complement your brand. These elements should be consistently used across all platforms to create a unified look and feel.
5. **Tone of Voice:**
    - Your brand's tone of voice is how you communicate with your audience. It should reflect your brand's personality and values. Whether your tone is friendly and conversational or formal and authoritative, consistency is key. This tone should be evident in all written communications, from social media posts to customer service emails.

Positioning: Claiming Your Space in the Market

Brand positioning involves defining how you want your brand to be perceived in the minds of your target audience. It's about carving out a unique space in the market that differentiates you from competitors. Here's how to effectively position your brand:

1. **Identify Your Unique Value Proposition (UVP):**
   - Your UVP is the distinct value you offer that sets you apart from competitors. It's the answer to the question, "Why should customers choose you?" To define your UVP, consider what makes your products or services unique, the benefits they provide, and how they solve customer problems.
   - For instance, if you run an eco-friendly cleaning product company, your UVP might be: "Safe, sustainable cleaning solutions that protect your family and the planet."
2. **Understand Your Competitors:**
   - Conduct a competitive analysis to understand how other businesses in your industry position themselves. Identify gaps in the market and opportunities to differentiate your brand. Look at their strengths and weaknesses, and find ways to offer something different or better.
3. **Know Your Audience:**
   - Tailor your positioning to resonate with your target audience. Use the insights gained from your market research to understand their needs, preferences, and pain points. Your positioning should address these aspects and align with what matters most to your customers.
4. **Craft a Positioning Statement:**
   - A positioning statement succinctly defines your brand's unique place in the market. It typically includes your target audience, the category you operate in, the benefit you

provide, and the reason to believe in your brand. Here's a template to get you started:
- "For [target audience], [brand] is the [category] that [benefit] because [reason to believe]."
  - Using our eco-friendly cleaning product company example: "For environmentally-conscious families, GreenClean is the cleaning solution that offers powerful, safe, and sustainable cleaning because it's made from all-natural ingredients."

5. **Communicate Consistently:**
   - Ensure that your brand positioning is consistently communicated across all marketing channels and customer touchpoints. From your website and social media to advertising and packaging, every interaction should reinforce your brand's unique position.

Real-Life Example:

Let's consider Warby Parker, a company that disrupted the eyewear industry with its unique brand identity and positioning. Warby Parker's clean, minimalist design and approachable tone of voice resonated with a younger, fashion-forward audience. Their UVP—high-quality, stylish eyewear at a fraction of the traditional cost, along with a commitment to social responsibility—set them apart from established competitors.

Warby Parker's branding extended beyond visuals. Their engaging storytelling, direct-to-consumer model, and innovative Home Try-On program aligned with their positioning as an affordable, customer-centric alternative in the eyewear market. This cohesive branding strategy helped Warby Parker build a loyal customer base and become a household name.

Conclusion:

Building a strong brand identity and positioning your brand effectively are crucial steps in differentiating your business and connecting with your target audience. By carefully crafting your brand's visual and emotional elements and clearly defining your unique value proposition, you can create a compelling brand that stands out in the marketplace. Remember, consistency is key—every touchpoint should reflect your brand's identity and reinforce your positioning.

1.2.2. Effective Branding Strategies

Effective branding strategies are essential for establishing a strong presence in the market and fostering customer loyalty. With the right strategies, you can communicate your brand's value, connect with your audience, and build lasting relationships. Let's explore some proven branding strategies that can help your small business thrive.

1. Develop a Consistent Brand Voice and Visual Identity

Consistency is the cornerstone of effective branding. Your brand voice and visual identity should be uniform across all channels to create a cohesive and recognizable brand image.

- **Brand Voice:**

- Your brand voice is how you communicate with your audience. It should reflect your brand's personality and values. Whether your tone is casual and friendly or professional and authoritative, maintain consistency in all communications. This includes social media posts, email newsletters, customer service interactions, and advertising campaigns.
- For example, if your brand is playful and youthful, use a conversational tone with informal language and humor. On the other hand, if your brand is more serious and professional, maintain a formal and respectful tone.

- **Visual Identity:**
  - Your visual identity includes your logo, color palette, typography, and imagery. Ensure these elements are used consistently across all marketing materials, including your website, social media, packaging, and promotional materials. Consistent visuals help reinforce brand recognition and build trust with your audience.

2. Tell Your Brand Story

Storytelling is a powerful branding strategy that helps humanize your brand and connect with customers on an emotional level. Share your brand's origin story, mission, and values. Highlight the journey, challenges, and successes that have shaped your business.

- **Authenticity:**

- Be genuine and transparent in your storytelling. Authentic stories resonate more with audiences and build a deeper connection. Share the passion and purpose behind your brand, and let your customers see the real people behind the business.
- For instance, if you started your business in your garage with a mission to provide eco-friendly products, share that journey. Explain why sustainability is important to you and how it influences your business practices.

- **Customer Stories:**
  - Include stories from your customers to showcase how your products or services have positively impacted their lives. User-generated content, testimonials, and case studies are excellent ways to highlight real-life experiences and build credibility.

3. Leverage Social Media

Social media is a vital tool for building and maintaining your brand presence. It allows you to engage with your audience, share your brand story, and showcase your products or services.

- **Engagement:**
  - Interact with your followers regularly by responding to comments, messages, and mentions. Engaging with your audience fosters a sense of community and loyalty. Ask questions, conduct polls, and encourage

user-generated content to boost engagement.
    - For example, if you run a fashion brand, you can create a branded hashtag and encourage customers to share photos of themselves wearing your products. Reposting user-generated content on your social media channels can further strengthen your brand community.
- **Content Strategy:**
    - Develop a content strategy that aligns with your brand values and resonates with your target audience. Share a mix of content types, including behind-the-scenes glimpses, product highlights, educational posts, and customer stories. Visual content, such as images and videos, tends to perform well on social media and can effectively convey your brand message.

4. Offer Exceptional Customer Experiences

Exceptional customer experiences are crucial for building a strong brand. Positive interactions with your brand create loyal customers who are likely to become brand advocates.

- **Customer Service:**
    - Provide excellent customer service by being responsive, helpful, and empathetic. Address customer inquiries and issues promptly and go the extra mile to exceed their expectations. Personalize your interactions to make customers feel valued and appreciated.

- o For instance, if a customer has a problem with their order, resolve the issue quickly and consider offering a small discount or freebie as a gesture of goodwill.
- **Consistency:**
  - o Ensure that every touchpoint with your brand, from your website and social media to in-store experiences and customer support, is consistent and reflects your brand values. Consistent, positive experiences build trust and loyalty.

5. Collaborate with Influencers and Brand Ambassadors

Partnering with influencers and brand ambassadors can amplify your brand's reach and credibility. Choose individuals who align with your brand values and have a genuine connection with your target audience.

- **Influencer Marketing:**
  - o Collaborate with influencers who can authentically promote your products or services to their followers. Influencers can create engaging content, provide reviews, and share personal experiences with your brand.
  - o For example, if you sell fitness apparel, partnering with fitness influencers who share workout routines and lifestyle tips can help you reach a broader audience and build credibility.
- **Brand Ambassadors:**

- Develop a brand ambassador program where loyal customers and fans can represent your brand. Brand ambassadors can help spread the word about your products, participate in events, and create user-generated content.

Conclusion:

Effective branding strategies are essential for building a strong, recognizable, and trusted brand. By developing a consistent brand voice and visual identity, telling your brand story, leveraging social media, offering exceptional customer experiences, and collaborating with influencers, you can create a powerful brand that resonates with your audience and drives business success. Remember, branding is an ongoing process that requires dedication, creativity, and a deep understanding of your customers.

Chapter 2

2. Effective Marketing Strategies

Marketing is the lifeblood of any small business. It's the bridge that connects your products or services to your target audience. Effective marketing strategies not only attract new customers but also build loyalty and drive long-term success. In this chapter, we will delve into various marketing techniques and strategies that can elevate your business and help you stand out in a crowded marketplace.

Imagine your business as a lighthouse, guiding customers through the fog of countless options to your door. Marketing is the light that shines brightly, making your business visible and appealing. Whether you're using traditional methods or leveraging digital platforms, the goal is to communicate your value proposition clearly and compellingly to the right audience.

We will explore the essentials of digital marketing, from social media and content marketing to email campaigns and search engine optimization (SEO). Each of these tools has the potential to significantly boost your online presence and engage with your audience in meaningful ways. Additionally, we'll discuss traditional marketing techniques, such as direct mail campaigns and local events, which remain powerful in creating personal connections and community engagement.

As we navigate through these strategies, you'll find practical advice, real-life examples, and actionable steps to implement in your own business. By the end of this chapter, you will have a comprehensive toolkit of marketing strategies tailored to your unique needs and goals, ready to attract, engage, and retain your customers.

Get ready to illuminate the path to your business with effective marketing strategies that not only reach your target audience but also resonate with them deeply, creating lasting connections and driving your business toward sustained success.

2.1. Digital Marketing Essentials

2.1.1. Social Media Marketing

Social media marketing is a powerful tool for small businesses, providing a cost-effective way to reach and engage with your target audience. With billions of users across various platforms, social media offers unparalleled opportunities to build brand awareness, foster customer relationships, and drive sales. Let's explore the essentials of social media marketing and how you can leverage it to grow your business.

Choosing the Right Platforms

Not all social media platforms are created equal, and each serves different purposes. The key is to choose the platforms that align with your business goals and where your target audience is most active.

- **Facebook:** Ideal for building a community and sharing a variety of content types, including posts, images, videos, and events. It's particularly useful

for local businesses looking to engage with their community.
- **Instagram:** Great for visually-driven businesses such as fashion, food, and travel. It's perfect for sharing high-quality images and videos, and leveraging features like Stories and IGTV to connect with your audience.
- **Twitter:** Best for real-time engagement and sharing news, updates, and short-form content. It's effective for brands that want to engage in conversations and trending topics.
- **LinkedIn:** Essential for B2B businesses and professional networking. It's the platform of choice for sharing industry insights, company news, and professional content.
- **Pinterest:** Ideal for businesses in niches like DIY, crafts, home decor, and lifestyle. It's a powerful platform for driving traffic to your website through visually appealing pins.

Creating Engaging Content

The cornerstone of successful social media marketing is creating content that resonates with your audience. Here are some tips for crafting engaging content:

1. **Know Your Audience:**
   - Understand the demographics, interests, and pain points of your audience. Tailor your content to address their needs and preferences. Use tools like Facebook Insights and Instagram Analytics to gather data on your followers.
2. **Mix Content Types:**

- Diversify your content to keep your audience engaged. Use a mix of images, videos, stories, live streams, and written posts. For example, a bakery could share mouth-watering photos of their products, behind-the-scenes videos of the baking process, customer testimonials, and live Q&A sessions with the baker.
3. **Tell Stories:**
   - People connect with stories. Share the journey of your business, the passion behind your products, and the experiences of your customers. Authentic storytelling creates an emotional connection and makes your brand more relatable.
4. **Use Visuals:**
   - High-quality visuals are essential on social media. Invest in good photography and graphic design to make your posts stand out. Tools like Canva can help you create professional-looking graphics without extensive design skills.
5. **Incorporate Hashtags:**
   - Hashtags increase the discoverability of your content. Research and use relevant hashtags to reach a broader audience. For example, a fitness studio might use hashtags like #FitnessJourney, #WorkoutMotivation, and #HealthyLiving.

Engaging with Your Audience

Social media is not just about broadcasting; it's about engaging in two-way conversations with your audience. Here's how to foster engagement:

1. **Respond Promptly:**
   - Reply to comments, messages, and mentions promptly. Show your audience that you value their input and are available to address their questions or concerns.
2. **Encourage Interaction:**
   - Ask questions, run polls, and encourage user-generated content. Create opportunities for your audience to participate in conversations and share their experiences. For example, a coffee shop could ask followers to share photos of their favorite coffee moments using a branded hashtag.
3. **Host Contests and Giveaways:**
   - Contests and giveaways are excellent for boosting engagement and attracting new followers. Ensure that the rules are clear and the prizes are relevant to your audience. For instance, a beauty brand might host a giveaway for a set of their best-selling products, encouraging followers to like, share, and tag friends to enter.
4. **Collaborate with Influencers:**
   - Partner with influencers who align with your brand values and have a genuine connection with your target audience. Influencers can create authentic content

that showcases your products and reaches a wider audience.

Measuring Success

To ensure your social media efforts are effective, track and analyze key performance metrics. Here are some important metrics to monitor:

1. **Engagement Rate:**
   - Measure likes, comments, shares, and saves to gauge how your content resonates with your audience. High engagement indicates that your content is valuable and interesting.
2. **Reach and Impressions:**
   - Reach refers to the number of unique users who see your content, while impressions are the total number of times your content is displayed. These metrics help you understand the visibility of your posts.
3. **Follower Growth:**
   - Track the growth of your followers over time. Steady growth indicates that your content strategy is attracting new audience members.
4. **Website Traffic:**
   - Use tools like Google Analytics to track how much traffic your social media channels drive to your website. Analyze which platforms and posts generate the most visits.
5. **Conversions:**

- Measure the number of actions taken by users, such as making a purchase, signing up for a newsletter, or downloading a resource. Conversions indicate the effectiveness of your social media efforts in achieving business goals.

Conclusion

Social media marketing is a dynamic and powerful tool for small businesses. By choosing the right platforms, creating engaging content, interacting with your audience, and measuring your success, you can harness the full potential of social media to grow your business. Remember, consistency and authenticity are key—stay true to your brand, and your audience will follow.

2.1.2. Content Marketing

Content marketing is a strategic approach focused on creating and distributing valuable, relevant, and consistent content to attract and engage a clearly defined audience. For small businesses, content marketing is an effective way to build brand awareness, establish authority, and drive customer loyalty. Let's explore the key elements of a successful content marketing strategy and how to implement them.

Why Content Marketing Matters

Content marketing goes beyond traditional advertising by providing value to your audience without directly selling. It builds trust and credibility, positioning your brand as a thought leader in your industry. When done right, content marketing can generate leads, improve customer retention, and boost your search engine rankings.

Developing a Content Strategy

A well-defined content strategy is the foundation of effective content marketing. Here's how to create one:

1. **Set Clear Goals:**
    - Start by identifying what you want to achieve with your content marketing efforts. Common goals include increasing brand awareness, driving website traffic, generating leads, and boosting sales. Having clear objectives helps guide your content creation and measure success.
2. **Understand Your Audience:**
    - Know who your target audience is and what content they find valuable. Use buyer personas to identify their needs, preferences, and pain points. This understanding allows you to tailor your content to address their specific interests.
3. **Conduct a Content Audit:**
    - Review your existing content to identify what's working and what's not. Determine which topics resonate with your audience and which formats (blogs, videos, infographics) are most effective. A content audit helps you build on your strengths and fill in any gaps.
4. **Create a Content Plan:**
    - Develop a content calendar outlining what content you will create, when you will

publish it, and where it will be distributed. A well-structured plan ensures consistent content production and distribution, keeping your audience engaged.

Types of Content

Diverse content types can cater to different audience preferences and enhance your overall strategy. Here are some popular content formats:

1. **Blog Posts:**
   - Blogging is a cornerstone of content marketing. Regular blog posts on topics relevant to your audience can drive traffic to your website, improve SEO, and establish your expertise. For example, if you run a gardening store, blog about seasonal planting tips, garden maintenance, and DIY projects.
2. **Videos:**
   - Video content is highly engaging and shareable. It can include tutorials, product demonstrations, behind-the-scenes footage, and customer testimonials. Platforms like YouTube and social media are excellent for distributing video content.
3. **Infographics:**
   - Infographics present information visually, making complex data easy to understand and share. They are particularly effective for explaining processes, presenting statistics, and summarizing research findings.
4. **E-books and Whitepapers:**

- These in-depth resources provide valuable information on specific topics. E-books and whitepapers can be used to generate leads by offering them in exchange for contact information.
5. **Podcasts:**
    - Podcasts are a growing content format that allows you to share insights, interviews, and stories through audio. They are convenient for your audience to consume on the go and can help build a loyal following.
6. **Social Media Posts:**
    - Short, engaging content on social media platforms can drive traffic, increase engagement, and enhance brand visibility. Use a mix of text, images, and videos to keep your social media content fresh and interesting.

Content Creation Tips

Creating high-quality content consistently is key to a successful content marketing strategy. Here are some tips to help you produce compelling content:

1. **Focus on Quality Over Quantity:**
    - It's better to produce fewer pieces of high-quality content than to churn out a large volume of mediocre content. High-quality content is more likely to be shared, linked to, and appreciated by your audience.
2. **Be Authentic:**

- Authenticity builds trust. Share your unique perspective, experiences, and expertise. Don't be afraid to show the human side of your business through stories and personal anecdotes.

3. **Provide Value:**
     - Your content should address your audience's needs and solve their problems. Provide actionable insights, practical tips, and useful information that your audience can apply.

4. **Use Attention-Grabbing Headlines:**
     - Headlines are the first thing your audience sees, so make them compelling. Use clear, concise, and intriguing headlines that encourage people to read more.

5. **Optimize for SEO:**
     - Incorporate relevant keywords naturally into your content to improve your search engine rankings. Use tools like Google Keyword Planner to identify popular search terms related to your business.

Distributing Your Content

Creating great content is only half the battle; you also need an effective distribution strategy to reach your audience. Here are some ways to distribute your content:

1. **Social Media:**
     - Share your content across your social media channels to increase visibility and engagement. Tailor your posts to each platform's unique audience and format.

2. **Email Marketing:**
    - Use email newsletters to distribute your content directly to subscribers. Segment your email list to send targeted content based on your audience's interests and behaviors.
3. **Content Syndication:**
    - Partner with other websites, blogs, and online publications to syndicate your content. This can expand your reach and attract new audiences.
4. **Guest Blogging:**
    - Write guest posts for other blogs in your industry. This helps you reach a broader audience and build backlinks to your website.

Measuring Success

To ensure your content marketing efforts are effective, track and analyze key performance metrics:

1. **Website Traffic:**
    - Monitor the number of visitors to your website and identify which content drives the most traffic.
2. **Engagement:**
    - Measure likes, shares, comments, and time spent on your content to gauge how well it resonates with your audience.
3. **Lead Generation:**
    - Track the number of leads generated through content offers like e-books and webinars.

4. **Conversion Rates:**
   - Measure how many visitors take desired actions, such as making a purchase or signing up for a newsletter.

Conclusion

Content marketing is a powerful way to connect with your audience, build trust, and drive business growth. By developing a clear strategy, creating valuable content, and distributing it effectively, you can establish your brand as an industry leader and achieve your business goals. Remember, the key to successful content marketing is consistency, authenticity, and a deep understanding of your audience's needs.

2.2. Traditional Marketing Techniques

2.2.1. Direct Mail Campaigns

In an age dominated by digital marketing, traditional marketing techniques like direct mail campaigns still hold significant value. Direct mail can create a tangible connection with your audience, offering a personal touch that digital channels often lack. When executed effectively, direct mail campaigns can drive engagement, build brand loyalty, and generate sales. Let's explore how to design and implement successful direct mail campaigns for your small business.

The Power of Direct Mail

Direct mail has several advantages that make it a compelling marketing tool:

- **Tangibility:** Physical mail can create a lasting impression. A well-designed piece of direct mail can capture attention and be kept for future reference.
- **Personalization:** Direct mail can be highly personalized, addressing recipients by name and tailoring messages to their specific needs and preferences.
- **Targeting:** You can precisely target your direct mail campaigns based on demographics, geography, purchasing behavior, and more.
- **Higher Engagement:** Studies show that direct mail often has higher engagement rates compared to digital ads, as people tend to review their mail more thoroughly.

Designing Your Direct Mail Campaign

1. **Define Your Objectives:**
   - Clearly outline what you aim to achieve with your direct mail campaign. Common objectives include increasing sales, driving traffic to your website or physical store, promoting a new product or service, or building brand awareness.
2. **Identify Your Target Audience:**
   - Use customer data and market research to define your target audience. Segment your mailing list based on relevant criteria such as age, income, location, and purchasing behavior. The more specific your targeting, the more effective your campaign will be.
3. **Craft a Compelling Offer:**
   - An enticing offer is crucial for driving response. This could be a discount, a

limited-time promotion, a free sample, or an exclusive invitation. Ensure the offer provides real value to your audience and is easy to understand and redeem.
4. **Create an Engaging Design:**
    - Your direct mail piece should be visually appealing and professionally designed. Use high-quality images, clear fonts, and a clean layout. Include your brand logo and colors to maintain brand consistency. The design should guide the recipient's eye to the key elements, such as the offer, call to action, and contact information.
5. **Personalize Your Message:**
    - Personalization can significantly boost response rates. Address the recipient by name and tailor the message to their interests and behavior. Use variable data printing to customize different elements of the mail piece based on the recipient's profile.
6. **Include a Clear Call to Action (CTA):**
    - Your CTA should be prominent and compelling. Tell the recipient exactly what you want them to do, whether it's visiting your website, calling a phone number, or bringing the mail piece to your store. Include any necessary details like offer expiration dates or special codes.

Executing Your Direct Mail Campaign

1. **Choose the Right Format:**

- Direct mail comes in various formats, including postcards, letters, brochures, catalogs, and flyers. Choose the format that best suits your message and budget. Postcards are cost-effective and great for short, impactful messages, while letters and brochures can provide more detailed information.
2. **Print and Production:**
    - Partner with a reliable print service to ensure high-quality production. Consider options like glossy finishes, embossed elements, or die-cut shapes to make your mail piece stand out. Ensure your design files are print-ready and proofed to avoid errors.
3. **Mailing List Management:**
    - Maintain an up-to-date and accurate mailing list. Use list-cleaning services to remove duplicates, correct addresses, and update records. Segment your list as needed to match your targeting criteria.
4. **Timing and Frequency:**
    - Plan the timing of your mail drop to coincide with relevant events, seasons, or promotions. Decide on the frequency of your mailings based on your objectives and budget. Consistent mailings can keep your brand top of mind, but avoid overloading your recipients.

Measuring Success

To gauge the effectiveness of your direct mail campaign, track and analyze key performance metrics:

1. **Response Rate:**
   - Measure the percentage of recipients who take the desired action in response to your mail piece. This could be visiting your website, making a purchase, or redeeming a coupon.
2. **Conversion Rate:**
   - Track the percentage of respondents who complete the intended action, such as making a purchase. This helps you understand the direct impact of your campaign on sales.
3. **Return on Investment (ROI):**
   - Calculate the ROI by comparing the revenue generated from the campaign to the total costs incurred. A positive ROI indicates a successful campaign.
4. **Customer Feedback:**
   - Gather feedback from customers who responded to your direct mail. This can provide insights into what elements of the campaign were most effective and areas for improvement.

Real-Life Example:

Consider a local bookstore aiming to boost sales during the holiday season. They designed a beautifully crafted postcard featuring a festive design and an exclusive 20% discount on all purchases. The postcard included a personalized message addressing recipients by name and inviting them to a special holiday event at the store. The CTA encouraged recipients to bring the postcard to the event to redeem their discount.

The bookstore carefully segmented their mailing list to target loyal customers and local residents who had previously shown interest in book-related events. They timed the mail drop to arrive a week before the event, creating anticipation and urgency.

The campaign resulted in a significant increase in foot traffic and sales during the event. The personalized touch and compelling offer resonated with recipients, leading to a high response and conversion rate. The bookstore not only achieved its sales goals but also strengthened its relationship with the community.

Conclusion

Direct mail campaigns offer a unique and effective way to connect with your audience, providing a tangible and personal touch that digital marketing often lacks. By carefully designing your mail piece, targeting the right audience, and measuring your results, you can create successful direct mail campaigns that drive engagement and generate positive results for your small business.

2.2.2. NETWORKING AND EVENTS

Networking and events are powerful traditional marketing techniques that can significantly enhance your small business's visibility, credibility, and customer relationships. These face-to-face interactions provide unique opportunities to connect with potential clients, partners, and industry influencers. Let's delve into how you can effectively leverage networking and events to grow your business.

The Importance of Networking

Networking is about building relationships and creating a strong support system within your industry. It allows you to exchange ideas, gain insights, and establish connections that can lead to new business opportunities.

1. **Identify Networking Opportunities:**
    - Attend industry conferences, trade shows, local business meetups, and professional associations. These events are prime opportunities to meet like-minded individuals and potential clients.
    - Join online networking groups on platforms like LinkedIn. Participate in discussions and connect with professionals in your field.
2. **Prepare Your Elevator Pitch:**
    - An elevator pitch is a concise, compelling introduction that summarizes who you are, what your business does, and what makes it unique. Practice delivering your pitch confidently and naturally.
    - For example, if you own a digital marketing agency, yours might be: "Hi, I'm Jane, founder of Bright Spark Digital. We help small businesses boost their online presence through targeted social media campaigns and SEO strategies."
3. **Bring Business Cards:**
    - Business cards are a simple yet effective networking tool. Ensure your cards are

professional and include essential contact information. Distribute them generously at events.

4. **Engage in Meaningful Conversations:**
   - Focus on building genuine connections rather than just promoting your business. Ask questions, listen actively, and show interest in others' experiences and challenges. This approach fosters trust and rapport.

5. **Follow Up:**
   - After networking events, follow up with the people you met. Send a personalized email or connect on LinkedIn, referencing your conversation and expressing interest in staying in touch. This step solidifies the connection and keeps you top of mind.

Leveraging Events for Marketing

Hosting and participating in events can be a highly effective way to showcase your expertise, attract new customers, and strengthen existing relationships.

1. **Host Your Own Events:**
   - Organize workshops, seminars, or product launch events. Hosting events positions you as an industry leader and provides a platform to demonstrate your products or services.
   - For example, if you run a fitness studio, you could host a free community workout session or a wellness workshop. These events attract potential clients and give

them a firsthand experience of what you offer.

2. **Participate in Trade Shows and Expos:**
   - Trade shows and expos are excellent venues for reaching a large, targeted audience. Set up an engaging booth with eye-catching displays, product samples, and interactive elements.
   - Ensure your staff is knowledgeable and approachable. Collect contact information from visitors and follow up with them after the event.

3. **Collaborate with Other Businesses:**
   - Partnering with complementary businesses for co-hosted events can expand your reach and enhance your credibility. For instance, a local bakery and a coffee shop could co-host a "Coffee and Pastries Tasting Event."
   - This collaboration can attract customers from both businesses and create a more substantial impact.

4. **Utilize Speaking Engagements:**
   - Speaking at industry conferences, panels, or webinars positions you as an expert in your field. Share valuable insights, case studies, and actionable tips that highlight your expertise.
   - Prepare thoroughly and engage your audience with compelling stories and interactive elements. Leave time for questions to foster a dynamic and engaging session.

5. **Engage in Community Events:**

- Participating in or sponsoring local community events can boost your brand's visibility and reputation. Support charity runs, festivals, or school events to show your commitment to the community.
- For example, a local bookstore could sponsor a reading corner at a community fair, providing books and activities for children. This involvement not only enhances brand awareness but also builds goodwill.

Maximizing Event Impact

To ensure your networking and event efforts are effective, implement strategies to maximize their impact:

1. **Promote Your Participation:**
   - Use social media, email newsletters, and your website to promote your participation in upcoming events. Highlight what attendees can expect and any special offers or activities you'll provide.
   - Create event-specific hashtags and encourage attendees to share their experiences on social media.
2. **Capture Leads:**
   - Use sign-up sheets, business card collections, or digital tools like QR codes to capture contact information from event attendees. Offer incentives, such as a chance to win a prize or access to exclusive content, to encourage sign-ups.
3. **Provide Valuable Takeaways:**

- Offer attendees something tangible to remember your business by, such as branded merchandise, informative brochures, or exclusive discounts. Ensure these items reflect your brand and provide value.

4. **Analyze and Learn:**
    - After each event, evaluate its success. Analyze metrics such as attendance, engagement, lead generation, and sales impact. Gather feedback from attendees to identify areas for improvement.
    - Use these insights to refine your approach and enhance the effectiveness of future events.

Conclusion

Networking and events are powerful tools in your marketing arsenal. By building genuine relationships, hosting and participating in engaging events, and leveraging these opportunities effectively, you can enhance your brand's visibility, establish credibility, and drive business growth. Remember, the key to successful networking and events is preparation, engagement, and follow-up. With these strategies, you can create lasting impressions and foster strong connections that benefit your business in the long run.

Chapter 3

3. Financial Management for Small Businesses

Effective financial management is the cornerstone of any successful small business. It encompasses everything from budgeting and forecasting to managing cash flow and expenses. In this chapter, we will explore the essential financial practices that will help you maintain a healthy bottom line and ensure your business's long-term viability.

Imagine your business as a ship navigating the vast ocean. Financial management is the navigation system that keeps you on course, helping you avoid obstacles and make informed decisions about where to steer next. Without it, even the most promising business can quickly find itself adrift, struggling to stay afloat.

We will start by examining the basics of budgeting and forecasting, two critical tools for planning your financial future. Understanding how to create a realistic budget and accurately forecast your financial performance can provide a clear roadmap for your business activities. Next, we'll delve into the intricacies of managing cash flow, ensuring that you have enough liquidity to cover your obligations and invest in growth opportunities.

Additionally, we'll cover practical tips for controlling expenses, maximizing revenue, and maintaining financial health. Real-life examples and actionable steps will illustrate how these principles can be applied to your small business, making complex financial concepts more approachable and manageable.

By the end of this chapter, you will have a solid foundation in financial management, empowering you to make informed decisions, optimize your resources, and achieve financial stability. Whether you're just starting out or looking to refine your financial strategies, these insights will be invaluable in steering your business toward sustained success.

3.1. BUDGETING AND FORECASTING

3.1.1. CREATING A REALISTIC BUDGET

Creating a realistic budget is one of the most important financial tasks for any small business. A well-constructed budget helps you allocate resources, plan for future expenses, and measure your financial performance. It serves as a financial roadmap, guiding your decisions and ensuring that your business remains on track. Let's explore the steps to create a realistic budget that supports your business goals.

1. Understand Your Revenue Sources

The first step in creating a budget is to understand and forecast your revenue. Identify all potential income streams and estimate how much revenue each will generate. This includes sales of products or services, investment income, grants, and any other sources of revenue.

- **Historical Data:** If your business has been operating for some time, use historical data to

predict future revenue. Look at past sales trends and seasonality to make informed projections.
- **Market Analysis:** For new businesses, market analysis can provide insights into potential revenue. Research your industry, competitors, and target market to estimate how much revenue you can realistically expect.

2. List Fixed and Variable Expenses

Next, list all your expenses. Categorize them into fixed and variable costs to understand where your money is going and where you can make adjustments.

- **Fixed Expenses:** These are regular, recurring costs that do not change significantly month to month. Examples include rent, utilities, salaries, insurance, and loan repayments. Knowing your fixed expenses helps you understand the baseline costs of running your business.
- **Variable Expenses:** These costs fluctuate based on your business activity. Examples include raw materials, shipping costs, marketing expenses, and sales commissions. Variable expenses can be adjusted based on your revenue and business needs.

3. Include One-Time and Unexpected Costs

Account for one-time and unexpected costs in your budget. These can include equipment purchases, software upgrades, and emergency repairs. Setting aside a contingency fund for unexpected expenses ensures that you are prepared for unforeseen events without derailing your financial stability.

4. Set Financial Goals

Define clear financial goals for your business. These goals should align with your overall business objectives and be specific, measurable, achievable, relevant, and time-bound (SMART). Examples of financial goals include:

- Increasing monthly sales by 10%
- Reducing operating costs by 5%
- Building a cash reserve equivalent to three months of expenses

Setting these goals gives you a target to work towards and a benchmark to measure your progress.

5. Create the Budget

With all the necessary information at hand, you can now create your budget. Use a spreadsheet or accounting software to organize your data. Here's a simple structure to follow:

- **Revenue:** List all revenue sources and their projected amounts.
- **Fixed Expenses:** List all fixed costs and their amounts.
- **Variable Expenses:** List all variable costs and their amounts.
- **One-Time Expenses:** Include any planned one-time costs.
- **Contingency Fund:** Allocate a portion of your budget for unexpected expenses.
- **Net Profit:** Calculate your net profit by subtracting total expenses from total revenue.

For example, if your projected monthly revenue is $10,000, your fixed expenses are $3,000, variable expenses are $2,000, and you set aside $500 for one-time expenses and $500 for a contingency fund, your net profit would be $4,000.

6. Monitor and Adjust Your Budget

Creating a budget is not a one-time task; it requires ongoing monitoring and adjustments. Regularly compare your actual financial performance against your budget to identify variances and understand their causes. Adjust your budget as necessary to reflect changes in your business environment, such as new revenue opportunities or increased costs.

- **Monthly Reviews:** Conduct monthly reviews of your financial performance. Analyze where you are over or under budget and make necessary adjustments. This proactive approach helps you stay on track and make informed financial decisions.
- **Use Financial Software:** Leverage accounting and budgeting software like QuickBooks, Xero, or FreshBooks to automate and streamline your budgeting process. These tools provide real-time insights and simplify financial management.

Real-Life Example:

Consider Emily, who runs a small bakery. When she first opened her business, Emily struggled with cash flow issues due to unpredictable expenses and revenue fluctuations. By creating a detailed budget, Emily was able to better manage her finances. She identified her fixed costs, such as rent and salaries, and her variable costs, like ingredients and packaging. Emily also set aside funds for equipment maintenance and unexpected repairs.

With a clear budget, Emily could forecast her monthly revenue based on past sales data and seasonal trends. She set financial goals, such as increasing her monthly sales by 15% through targeted marketing campaigns. By monitoring her budget regularly and adjusting for any variances, Emily improved her cash flow, reduced unnecessary expenses, and achieved her financial goals.

Conclusion

Creating a realistic budget is essential for the financial health and success of your small business. It provides a clear picture of your revenue and expenses, helps you set and achieve financial goals, and ensures that you are prepared for unexpected costs. By following these steps and regularly monitoring your budget, you can make informed financial decisions and steer your business towards sustained profitability.

3.1.2. Financial Forecasting Methods

Financial forecasting is the process of predicting your business's future financial performance based on historical data, market trends, and other relevant factors. Accurate forecasting helps you make informed decisions, plan for growth, and mitigate potential risks. Let's explore the essential financial forecasting methods and how to implement them effectively.

Why Financial Forecasting Matters

Financial forecasting provides several key benefits:

- **Informed Decision-Making:** Forecasting allows you to anticipate future financial conditions, helping you make strategic decisions regarding investments, expansions, and cost management.
- **Risk Management:** By predicting potential financial challenges, you can develop contingency plans to address them proactively.
- **Goal Setting and Performance Tracking:** Forecasts provide benchmarks for measuring your business's performance and progress towards financial goals.

Types of Financial Forecasting

There are various financial forecasting methods, each suited to different needs and contexts. Here are the most commonly used methods:

1. **Qualitative Forecasting:**
    - This method relies on expert judgment and market research rather than numerical data. It's useful when historical data is limited or when entering new markets.
    - Techniques include the Delphi method (collecting and aggregating expert opinions) and market research surveys (gathering insights from potential customers and industry experts).
2. **Quantitative Forecasting:**
    - This method uses numerical data and statistical models to predict future financial

performance. It's suitable for businesses with sufficient historical data.
- Techniques include:
    - **Time Series Analysis:** Analyzing historical data to identify patterns and trends that can be projected into the future. For example, using past monthly sales data to forecast future sales.
    - **Regression Analysis:** Examining the relationship between variables (e.g., advertising spend and sales) to predict future outcomes.

3. **Causal Forecasting:**
   - This method identifies cause-and-effect relationships between variables. It's useful for understanding how specific factors influence financial performance.
   - For example, a retailer might use causal forecasting to predict sales based on factors like economic conditions, consumer confidence, and marketing efforts.

4. **Simulation Forecasting:**
   - This method uses computer models to simulate various scenarios and their potential financial outcomes. It's helpful for evaluating the impact of different strategies and decisions.
   - Techniques include Monte Carlo simulations, which generate a range of possible outcomes based on random variables.

Implementing Financial Forecasting

Here's a step-by-step guide to implementing financial forecasting for your small business:

1. **Gather Relevant Data:**
   - Collect historical financial data, including sales, expenses, cash flow, and profits. The more detailed and accurate your data, the better your forecasts will be.
2. **Choose the Right Method:**
   - Select a forecasting method that aligns with your business needs and available data. For example, use time series analysis if you have ample historical data or qualitative methods if you're entering a new market.
3. **Analyze Historical Data:**
   - Examine past financial performance to identify trends, patterns, and seasonal variations. Look for factors that have historically influenced your business, such as economic conditions, market trends, and internal changes.
4. **Develop Assumptions:**
   - Based on your analysis, develop assumptions about future performance. Consider factors like market growth, competition, pricing strategies, and marketing efforts. Ensure your assumptions are realistic and based on credible information.
5. **Create Forecast Models:**
   - Build financial models using your chosen forecasting method. Spreadsheet software like Excel can be helpful for creating detailed financial models. Include

projections for revenue, expenses, cash flow, and profits.

6. **Validate and Adjust Forecasts:**
    - Validate your forecasts by comparing them against actual performance over time. Adjust your models as needed to improve accuracy. Regularly review and update your forecasts to reflect changing conditions and new information.

Practical Example:

Consider Laura, who owns a boutique clothing store. To forecast her future sales, Laura uses time series analysis. She gathers three years of monthly sales data and identifies seasonal patterns, such as higher sales during the holiday season and slower months in early spring.

Using this historical data, Laura creates a time series model to project her sales for the upcoming year. She also considers external factors like economic conditions and upcoming marketing campaigns. Laura's forecast helps her plan inventory purchases, schedule staff, and allocate her marketing budget effectively.

To validate her forecast, Laura compares her projected sales with actual sales each month. She notices that a new competitor affects her summer sales, so she adjusts her model to account for this change. By continually refining her forecast, Laura gains valuable insights that help her make informed decisions and maintain financial stability.

Conclusion

Financial forecasting is a critical tool for small business success. By predicting future financial performance, you can make strategic decisions, manage risks, and achieve your business goals. Whether you use qualitative, quantitative, causal, or simulation forecasting methods, the key is to gather accurate data, develop realistic assumptions, and regularly review and adjust your forecasts. With effective financial forecasting, you can navigate the uncertainties of business with confidence and clarity.

3.2. Managing Cash Flow

3.2.1. Cash Flow Analysis

Managing cash flow is crucial for the survival and growth of any small business. Cash flow refers to the movement of money in and out of your business, and effectively managing it ensures you have enough liquidity to meet your obligations and invest in growth opportunities. Cash flow analysis involves examining your cash inflows and outflows to identify patterns, potential issues, and areas for improvement. Let's explore how to conduct a thorough cash flow analysis for your small business.

Understanding Cash Flow

Cash flow is categorized into three main types:

- **Operating Cash Flow:** Money generated from your core business operations, such as sales revenue and expenses related to producing goods or services.
- **Investing Cash Flow:** Money spent on or received from investments, such as purchasing equipment or selling assets.

- **Financing Cash Flow:** Money related to financing activities, such as loans, repayments, and equity investments.

A positive cash flow indicates that more money is coming into your business than going out, which is essential for sustaining operations and funding growth. Conversely, negative cash flow can signal financial trouble and requires immediate attention.

Steps to Conduct Cash Flow Analysis

1. **Prepare a Cash Flow Statement:**
    - A cash flow statement is a financial document that provides a detailed account of cash inflows and outflows over a specific period. It helps you track the sources and uses of cash in your business.
    - Use accounting software like QuickBooks, Xero, or FreshBooks to generate accurate cash flow statements. If you prefer manual tracking, create a spreadsheet with sections for operating, investing, and financing activities.
2. **Collect Financial Data:**
    - Gather all relevant financial data, including bank statements, sales records, invoices, and expense receipts. Ensure the data is complete and up-to-date to get an accurate picture of your cash flow.
3. **Analyze Operating Cash Flow:**
    - Start by examining your operating cash flow. Identify your primary sources of revenue and major operating expenses.

Look for trends in sales, seasonal variations, and any discrepancies in your income and expenses.
- For example, if you notice a dip in sales during certain months, consider implementing strategies to boost sales during those periods, such as promotions or targeted marketing campaigns.

4. **Evaluate Investing Cash Flow:**
   - Next, review your investing cash flow. Assess the impact of major purchases or sales of assets on your overall cash flow. Determine if these investments are yielding the expected returns and if they are aligned with your business goals.
   - For instance, if you recently invested in new equipment, evaluate how it has affected your productivity and whether it has contributed to increased revenue.

5. **Examine Financing Cash Flow:**
   - Finally, analyze your financing cash flow. Review any loans, repayments, equity investments, or dividend payments. Ensure that your financing activities support your business's long-term financial health.
   - If you have outstanding loans, consider the interest rates and repayment terms. Explore options to refinance or consolidate loans to improve cash flow.

Identifying Cash Flow Issues

As you conduct your cash flow analysis, look for potential issues that could impact your financial stability:

1. **Late Payments from Customers:**
   - Late payments can disrupt your cash flow and create liquidity problems. Implement a clear credit policy and follow up on overdue invoices promptly. Consider offering discounts for early payments or using invoice factoring services.
2. **High Operating Costs:**
   - Excessive operating costs can drain your cash reserves. Identify areas where you can reduce expenses without compromising quality. Negotiate better terms with suppliers, optimize inventory levels, and streamline operations to cut costs.
3. **Seasonal Variations:**
   - Many businesses experience seasonal fluctuations in cash flow. Plan for these variations by building a cash reserve during peak periods to cover expenses during slower months. Diversify your product or service offerings to create more stable revenue streams.
4. **Unplanned Expenses:**
   - Unexpected costs can quickly deplete your cash reserves. Establish a contingency fund to cover emergencies and avoid financial strain. Regularly review your budget and adjust it to account for unforeseen expenses.

Improving Cash Flow Management

Effective cash flow management involves proactive planning and regular monitoring. Here are some strategies to improve your cash flow:

1. **Forecast Future Cash Flow:**
   - Create cash flow forecasts to predict your future cash needs and identify potential shortfalls. Use historical data and market trends to make informed projections. Regularly update your forecasts to reflect changes in your business environment.
2. **Enhance Revenue Collection:**
   - Streamline your billing and payment processes to speed up revenue collection. Use online invoicing and payment systems to reduce delays. Offer multiple payment options to make it easier for customers to pay on time.
3. **Optimize Inventory Management:**
   - Efficient inventory management can free up cash tied in stock. Implement inventory control systems to track stock levels, reduce overstocking, and prevent stockouts. Use just-in-time inventory practices to minimize holding costs.
4. **Control Operating Expenses:**
   - Monitor and control your operating expenses to maintain a healthy cash flow. Review your expenses regularly and identify areas for cost savings. Implement cost-effective practices and negotiate with suppliers for better rates.

Real-Life Example:

Consider Tom, who owns a small printing business. By conducting a thorough cash flow analysis, Tom discovered that late payments from customers were causing cash flow issues. He implemented an online invoicing system with automated reminders, which improved payment timeliness. Additionally, Tom identified high costs in his supply chain and negotiated better terms with his suppliers, reducing his operating expenses.

Tom also created a cash flow forecast to plan for seasonal variations. During peak periods, he set aside extra cash to cover expenses during slower months. By taking these steps, Tom improved his cash flow management, ensuring he had sufficient liquidity to sustain and grow his business.

Conclusion

Cash flow analysis is a vital practice for maintaining the financial health of your small business. By understanding your cash inflows and outflows, identifying potential issues, and implementing strategies to improve cash flow management, you can ensure your business remains financially stable and positioned for growth. Regularly monitor your cash flow and make adjustments as needed to navigate the dynamic business environment with confidence.

3.2.2. Strategies to Improve Cash Flow

Improving cash flow is essential for the sustainability and growth of your small business. Positive cash flow ensures that you can meet your financial obligations, invest in opportunities, and navigate unexpected challenges. Here are some effective strategies to enhance your cash flow management and maintain a healthy financial position.

1. Accelerate Receivables

Speeding up the collection of receivables can significantly improve your cash flow. Here are some tactics to achieve this:

- **Invoice Promptly:** Send invoices immediately after providing a service or delivering a product. The sooner you invoice, the sooner you can expect payment.
- **Offer Early Payment Discounts:** Encourage customers to pay their invoices early by offering a small discount. For example, a 2% discount for payments made within 10 days can incentivize faster payments.
- **Implement Online Payments:** Use online payment systems to make it easier for customers to pay. Platforms like PayPal, Square, and Stripe offer quick and secure payment options that can expedite the payment process.
- **Automate Invoicing and Reminders:** Use accounting software to automate invoicing and set up automatic payment reminders for overdue accounts. This reduces the time spent on manual follow-ups and helps ensure timely payments.

2. Optimize Inventory Management

Effective inventory management can free up cash tied up in unsold stock. Here are some strategies to optimize your inventory:

- **Just-In-Time (JIT) Inventory:** Adopt JIT inventory practices to reduce holding costs and minimize excess stock. Order inventory only when needed to

fulfill orders, reducing the amount of cash tied up in inventory.
- **Regular Inventory Audits:** Conduct regular audits to identify slow-moving or obsolete stock. Implement strategies to liquidate excess inventory, such as discounts or promotions.
- **Demand Forecasting:** Use historical sales data and market trends to forecast demand accurately. This helps you maintain optimal inventory levels and avoid overstocking or stockouts.

3. Extend Payables

While accelerating receivables, you can also improve cash flow by extending payables. Here's how:

- **Negotiate Longer Payment Terms:** Work with suppliers to negotiate longer payment terms, giving you more time to pay invoices without incurring penalties. For example, extending payment terms from 30 to 45 days can provide additional cash flow flexibility.
- **Consolidate Suppliers:** Consolidate your purchasing with fewer suppliers to leverage better payment terms and discounts. Building strong relationships with key suppliers can lead to more favorable terms.

4. Control Operating Expenses

Managing your operating expenses is crucial for maintaining positive cash flow. Here are some cost-control strategies:

- **Review and Cut Unnecessary Expenses:** Regularly review your expenses and identify areas where you can cut costs. Look for subscriptions, services, or utilities that you no longer need or can find cheaper alternatives for.
- **Outsource Non-Core Functions:** Outsource non-core business functions, such as accounting, IT, or marketing, to specialized firms. This can reduce overhead costs and allow you to focus on core business activities.
- **Energy Efficiency:** Implement energy-efficient practices to reduce utility costs. Simple measures like switching to LED lighting, using programmable thermostats, and conducting energy audits can lead to significant savings.

5. Increase Sales

Boosting sales is a direct way to improve cash flow. Here are some strategies to drive revenue growth:

- **Upsell and Cross-Sell:** Train your sales team to upsell and cross-sell to existing customers. Offering complementary products or higher-end options can increase the average transaction value.
- **Promotions and Discounts:** Run targeted promotions and discounts to attract new customers and encourage repeat purchases. Ensure that these promotions are well-planned to avoid eroding profit margins.
- **Expand Product or Service Offerings:** Diversify your product or service offerings to reach new customer segments and increase revenue streams.

Conduct market research to identify unmet needs and opportunities for expansion.

6. Manage Financing

Effective financing management can provide the necessary cash flow support during lean periods. Here are some options:

- **Line of Credit:** Establish a line of credit with your bank to provide quick access to funds when needed. This can be a valuable safety net for managing short-term cash flow gaps.
- **Invoice Financing:** Use invoice financing or factoring to access immediate cash based on your outstanding invoices. This can be particularly useful for businesses with long payment cycles.
- **Short-Term Loans:** Consider short-term loans to cover temporary cash flow shortages. Ensure that the loan terms are manageable and that you have a clear plan for repayment.

Real-Life Example:

Consider Sarah, who runs a small boutique. To improve her cash flow, Sarah implemented several strategies. She started by offering early payment discounts to her customers, which reduced the average payment time from 30 days to 15 days. She also optimized her inventory by adopting JIT practices, which reduced her holding costs and freed up cash.

Sarah negotiated longer payment terms with her suppliers, extending them from 30 days to 45 days, giving her more flexibility in managing her cash outflows. She reviewed her operating expenses and switched to a more cost-effective utility provider, cutting her monthly utility costs by 20%.

By implementing these strategies, Sarah not only improved her cash flow but also positioned her business for sustainable growth.

Conclusion

Improving cash flow requires a combination of accelerating receivables, optimizing inventory, extending payables, controlling expenses, increasing sales, and managing financing. By implementing these strategies, you can ensure a steady flow of cash into your business, enabling you to meet your obligations, invest in growth opportunities, and navigate financial challenges with confidence. Regularly review and adjust your cash flow management practices to adapt to changing business conditions and maintain financial stability.

Chapter 4

4. Leadership and Team Building

Leadership and team building are fundamental components of any successful small business. A strong leader not only drives the business forward but also inspires and empowers their team to achieve collective goals. In this chapter, we will delve into the essential traits of effective leadership and explore strategies for building a high-performing team.

Imagine your business as a ship navigating through the vast ocean of the marketplace. As the captain, your leadership skills determine the course, while your crew—your team—ensures that the ship sails smoothly and efficiently. Without strong leadership and a cohesive team, even the most promising ventures can struggle to reach their full potential.

We will begin by examining the key characteristics of effective leaders, such as vision, communication, empathy, and decisiveness. Understanding and cultivating these traits will help you guide your team with confidence and clarity. Next, we'll explore practical team-building strategies, from hiring the right talent and fostering a positive work culture to promoting collaboration and continuous learning.

Through real-life examples and actionable steps, this chapter will provide you with the tools and insights needed to enhance your leadership abilities and build a team that is motivated, engaged, and aligned with your business goals. By the end of this chapter, you will have a deeper understanding of how to lead with purpose and create an environment where your team can thrive.

Prepare to embark on a journey of personal and professional growth as we uncover the principles of effective leadership and the art of building a cohesive, high-performing team.

4.1. Effective Leadership Traits

4.1.1. Leading by Example

Leading by example is one of the most powerful leadership traits. It sets the tone for your team and creates a culture of accountability, trust, and respect. As a leader, your actions speak louder than words. By demonstrating the behaviors and attitudes you expect from your team, you inspire them to follow suit and uphold the standards you set. Let's explore what it means to lead by example and how you can implement this principle in your business.

The Importance of Leading by Example

Leading by example establishes credibility and trust. When your team sees that you are committed to the same standards and work ethic you expect from them, they are more likely to respect and follow your leadership. This approach fosters a positive and productive work environment where everyone is motivated to contribute their best.

Key Aspects of Leading by Example

1. **Demonstrate Integrity and Honesty:**

- Integrity and honesty are foundational to effective leadership. Always be truthful, transparent, and fair in your dealings with your team. Admit mistakes and take responsibility for your actions. When your team sees you acting with integrity, they are more likely to do the same.

2. **Exhibit a Strong Work Ethic:**
    - Show your commitment to hard work and excellence. Arrive on time, meet deadlines, and consistently deliver high-quality work. Your dedication and effort set a standard for your team to aspire to.

3. **Maintain a Positive Attitude:**
    - A positive attitude is contagious. Approach challenges with optimism and resilience. Encourage your team to see obstacles as opportunities for growth and learning. Your positive outlook can boost morale and inspire a can-do attitude among your team members.

4. **Communicate Effectively:**
    - Clear and open communication is essential for leading by example. Be approachable and actively listen to your team's concerns and ideas. Provide constructive feedback and acknowledge their contributions. Effective communication builds trust and fosters a collaborative environment.

5. **Practice Empathy and Compassion:**
    - Show empathy and compassion towards your team members. Understand their needs, challenges, and aspirations. Support them through difficult times and celebrate

their successes. When your team feels valued and understood, they are more likely to be loyal and motivated.

6. **Encourage Continuous Learning:**
   - Lead by example in personal and professional development. Pursue opportunities to learn and grow, and encourage your team to do the same. Share your knowledge and experiences to inspire others. A culture of continuous learning drives innovation and improvement.

Implementing Leading by Example in Your Business

1. **Set Clear Expectations:**
   - Clearly communicate your expectations regarding work quality, behavior, and values. Ensure that your team understands what is expected of them and why these standards are important. Align your actions with these expectations to reinforce their significance.

2. **Be Accessible and Approachable:**
   - Make yourself available to your team for support and guidance. Encourage open communication and create an environment where team members feel comfortable sharing their thoughts and concerns. Being accessible demonstrates your commitment to their success.

3. **Lead from the Front:**
   - Don't shy away from taking on challenging tasks or stepping into the trenches with your team. Show that you are willing to

work alongside them and share the workload. Leading from the front builds camaraderie and shows that you are part of the team, not just an overseer.

4. **Recognize and Reward Effort:**
   - Acknowledge the hard work and achievements of your team members. Provide positive reinforcement and reward their efforts. Recognition can take many forms, from verbal praise to formal awards. Recognizing effort reinforces positive behavior and motivates your team to continue striving for excellence.

5. **Foster a Culture of Accountability:**
   - Hold yourself and your team accountable for their actions and performance. Set a standard of accountability by admitting mistakes and correcting them. Encourage your team to take ownership of their responsibilities and learn from their experiences.

Real-Life Example:

Consider the story of John, who owns a small tech startup. John believes in leading by example and consistently demonstrates the values he wants to instill in his team. He arrives early to the office, works diligently, and maintains a positive attitude even during challenging times. John's transparency about the company's goals and his willingness to listen to his team's input fosters a culture of trust and collaboration.

When a critical project faced unexpected hurdles, John didn't just delegate tasks; he actively participated in brainstorming solutions and working late alongside his team to meet deadlines. His dedication and support motivated the team to push through the challenges and deliver exceptional results.

John's leadership by example has created a work environment where team members feel valued, respected, and motivated to excel. His company has experienced steady growth, driven by a cohesive and committed team.

Conclusion

Leading by example is a powerful way to inspire and influence your team. By demonstrating integrity, a strong work ethic, a positive attitude, effective communication, empathy, and a commitment to continuous learning, you set a standard for your team to follow. Implementing these principles in your business fosters a culture of trust, accountability, and excellence, driving your team and your business towards sustained success.

4.1.2. MOTIVATING YOUR TEAM

Motivating your team is crucial for maintaining high levels of productivity, creativity, and job satisfaction. A motivated team is more likely to go above and beyond, contributing to the overall success and growth of your business. As a leader, understanding what drives your team and implementing strategies to keep them motivated can make a significant difference. Let's explore some effective ways to motivate your team.

Understanding What Motivates Your Team

Before you can effectively motivate your team, it's essential to understand what drives them. Different individuals are motivated by different factors, which can include:

- **Intrinsic Motivation:** This comes from within and includes personal satisfaction, a sense of achievement, and the joy of performing the task itself. Employees motivated intrinsically often find fulfillment in the work they do and take pride in their contributions.
- **Extrinsic Motivation:** This is driven by external rewards such as bonuses, promotions, recognition, and benefits. Extrinsic motivators can be powerful but may need to be balanced with intrinsic motivators for long-term engagement.

Strategies to Motivate Your Team

1. **Set Clear Goals and Expectations:**
   - Clearly define and communicate your business goals and individual expectations. When team members understand what is expected of them and how their work contributes to the bigger picture, they are more likely to be motivated and aligned with the company's mission.
   - Use the SMART criteria (Specific, Measurable, Achievable, Relevant, Time-bound) to set clear and attainable goals.
2. **Provide Regular Feedback and Recognition:**
   - Regular feedback helps employees understand their strengths and areas for improvement. Constructive feedback should

be specific, actionable, and delivered in a supportive manner.
- Recognition is a powerful motivator. Acknowledge and celebrate individual and team achievements. This can be done through verbal praise, awards, public recognition, or even a simple thank-you note.

3. **Offer Opportunities for Growth and Development:**
   - Invest in your team's professional development by providing opportunities for training, learning, and advancement. Encourage employees to attend workshops, enroll in courses, and pursue certifications.
   - Promote from within whenever possible to show that hard work and dedication are rewarded with career growth.

4. **Foster a Positive Work Environment:**
   - Create a workplace culture that promotes positivity, collaboration, and respect. Encourage open communication and ensure that all team members feel heard and valued.
   - Implement initiatives that promote work-life balance, such as flexible working hours, remote work options, and wellness programs.

5. **Empower and Involve Your Team:**
   - Give your team members autonomy and trust them to take ownership of their tasks. Empowering employees to make decisions and take responsibility fosters a sense of pride and accountability.

- Involve your team in decision-making processes, especially those that affect their work. Seeking their input and valuing their opinions can boost morale and engagement.
6. **Provide the Right Tools and Resources:**
    - Ensure that your team has the necessary tools, resources, and support to perform their tasks efficiently. This includes up-to-date technology, adequate workspace, and access to information.
    - Address any obstacles or challenges that may hinder their productivity and find solutions to overcome them.
7. **Create a Sense of Purpose:**
    - Help your team understand the impact of their work and how it contributes to the company's mission and vision. A sense of purpose can be a significant motivator, driving employees to excel and stay committed.
    - Share success stories and customer feedback to highlight the positive outcomes of their efforts.

Real-Life Example:

Consider Sarah, who manages a small marketing team. Sarah noticed that her team's motivation was waning, so she implemented several strategies to boost their morale. She started by setting clear, achievable goals for each team member and regularly provided constructive feedback.

Sarah also introduced a monthly recognition program to celebrate individual and team accomplishments. She organized professional development workshops and encouraged her team to pursue additional training. To foster a positive work environment, Sarah implemented flexible working hours and remote work options, which helped improve work-life balance.

By involving her team in key decisions and providing them with the necessary tools and resources, Sarah empowered her employees to take ownership of their projects. She frequently shared customer success stories to remind her team of the impact of their work.

As a result of these efforts, Sarah's team became more motivated, engaged, and productive. The positive changes in the work environment led to higher job satisfaction and better overall performance.

Conclusion

Motivating your team is essential for achieving business success. By understanding what drives your employees and implementing strategies to keep them motivated, you can create a positive and productive work environment. Set clear goals, provide regular feedback and recognition, offer growth opportunities, foster a positive culture, empower your team, provide necessary resources, and create a sense of purpose. These efforts will help you build a motivated team that is committed to achieving collective goals and driving your business forward.

4.2. BUILDING A HIGH-PERFORMING TEAM

4.2.1. RECRUITMENT AND HIRING

Building a high-performing team starts with recruiting and hiring the right talent. The recruitment process is your opportunity to find individuals who not only have the necessary skills and experience but also align with your company's culture and values. Effective hiring practices ensure that you bring on board team members who can contribute to your business's success. Let's explore the steps to create a robust recruitment and hiring strategy.

Defining Your Needs

1. **Identify the Role:**
    - Clearly define the role you are hiring for. Create a detailed job description that outlines the responsibilities, required skills, qualifications, and any other pertinent details. This clarity helps attract the right candidates and sets clear expectations from the outset.
    - For example, if you're hiring a marketing manager, specify tasks such as developing marketing strategies, managing social media accounts, and analyzing campaign performance.
2. **Determine the Ideal Candidate:**
    - Identify the key attributes and qualifications you are looking for in an ideal candidate. Consider both technical skills and soft skills, such as communication, problem-solving, and teamwork. Think about the qualities that would complement your existing team and contribute to a positive work environment.

Attracting Candidates

1. **Craft a Compelling Job Posting:**
   - Write a job posting that is clear, engaging, and informative. Highlight the unique aspects of your company and the benefits of working with your team. Use inclusive language to attract a diverse pool of candidates.
   - Include information about your company culture, mission, and values. This helps potential candidates determine if they are a good fit for your organization.
2. **Use Multiple Channels:**
   - Post your job opening on various platforms to reach a broad audience. Use job boards like Indeed, LinkedIn, and Glassdoor, as well as industry-specific sites. Leverage your company's social media channels to spread the word.
   - Consider employee referrals as a valuable source of candidates. Encourage your team to refer qualified individuals and offer incentives for successful hires.

Screening and Interviewing

1. **Review Applications:**
   - Carefully review resumes and cover letters to shortlist candidates who meet the job requirements. Look for relevant experience, skills, and any red flags or inconsistencies. Use applicant tracking systems (ATS) to streamline the process.

2. **Conduct Initial Screenings:**
   - Perform initial phone or video screenings to assess candidates' qualifications and cultural fit. This step helps you narrow down the pool of applicants before moving to in-depth interviews.
   - During screenings, ask questions about their previous experience, why they are interested in the role, and their understanding of your company's mission and values.
3. **Prepare for Interviews:**
   - Develop a structured interview process with a set of standardized questions to ensure consistency and fairness. Include behavioral questions that require candidates to provide examples of how they have handled specific situations in the past.
   - Involve multiple team members in the interview process to get diverse perspectives on each candidate. This collaborative approach helps ensure that the candidate is a good fit for both the role and the team.
4. **Evaluate Soft Skills:**
   - Pay attention to candidates' soft skills during interviews. Assess their communication abilities, problem-solving skills, and cultural fit. These attributes are often just as important as technical skills in determining long-term success.

Making the Offer

1. **Check References:**
   - Before making an offer, conduct reference checks to verify candidates' work history and gain insights into their performance and work ethic. Ask specific questions about their strengths, areas for improvement, and overall suitability for the role.
2. **Make a Competitive Offer:**
   - Provide a competitive salary and benefits package that reflects the candidate's experience and the industry standards. Consider additional perks, such as flexible working hours, professional development opportunities, and health and wellness programs.
   - Clearly communicate the terms of the offer, including job responsibilities, expectations, and any probationary period. Be transparent and open to negotiations to ensure mutual satisfaction.

Onboarding New Hires

1. **Develop an Onboarding Plan:**
   - Create a comprehensive onboarding plan to help new hires integrate smoothly into your company. Include an orientation session, training programs, and introductions to key team members. Provide necessary resources and tools to help them get started.
   - Assign a mentor or buddy to support the new hire during their initial days. This helps

them feel welcome and provides a point of contact for any questions or concerns.
2. **Set Clear Expectations:**
    - Clearly communicate job responsibilities, performance expectations, and company policies. Provide regular feedback and support to help new hires adjust and succeed in their roles.
    - Schedule regular check-ins to address any challenges and ensure that the new hire is on track. This proactive approach helps identify and resolve issues early, promoting a positive onboarding experience.

Real-Life Example:

Consider Emma, who runs a small graphic design agency. To build a high-performing team, Emma started by defining the roles she needed to fill and the ideal attributes for each position. She crafted compelling job postings that highlighted her agency's creative culture and opportunities for growth.

Emma used multiple channels to attract candidates, including industry-specific job boards and social media. She screened applicants through initial video calls and conducted structured interviews with her team. By evaluating both technical skills and cultural fit, Emma was able to identify candidates who were not only talented but also aligned with her agency's values.

Before making offers, Emma conducted thorough reference checks and provided competitive compensation packages. She developed a comprehensive onboarding plan that included training, mentorship, and regular check-ins. As a result, Emma successfully built a cohesive and high-performing team that contributed to her agency's growth and success.

Conclusion

Recruiting and hiring the right talent is crucial for building a high-performing team. By clearly defining your needs, crafting compelling job postings, using multiple channels to attract candidates, conducting thorough screenings and interviews, making competitive offers, and providing effective onboarding, you can ensure that you bring on board individuals who will contribute positively to your business. A well-executed recruitment and hiring strategy sets the foundation for a motivated, skilled, and cohesive team that drives your business forward.

4.2.2. TRAINING AND DEVELOPMENT

Training and development are critical components of building a high-performing team. Investing in your employees' growth not only enhances their skills and knowledge but also boosts their motivation and loyalty. A well-structured training and development program can lead to increased productivity, innovation, and overall business success. Let's explore how to create effective training and development strategies for your small business.

The Importance of Training and Development

Training and development provide numerous benefits for both employees and employers:

- **Skill Enhancement:** Employees gain new skills and improve existing ones, leading to better performance and efficiency.
- **Employee Engagement:** Continuous learning opportunities keep employees engaged and motivated, reducing turnover rates.
- **Adaptability:** Well-trained employees can adapt to changes in the market or industry more quickly and effectively.
- **Innovation:** Training fosters creativity and innovation by exposing employees to new ideas and approaches.

Steps to Create an Effective Training and Development Program

1. **Assess Training Needs:**
    - Start by identifying the skills and knowledge gaps within your team. Conduct a thorough assessment through surveys, interviews, performance reviews, and feedback from team members.
    - Determine the specific areas where training is needed, whether it's technical skills, soft skills, or industry-specific knowledge.
2. **Set Clear Objectives:**
    - Define the goals of your training program. What do you want to achieve? Clear objectives help in designing targeted training sessions that address specific needs.
    - For example, if you aim to improve customer service, your objective might be to

enhance communication skills and problem-solving abilities.

3. **Develop a Training Plan:**
   - Create a comprehensive training plan that outlines the topics, methods, and schedule for training sessions. Include a mix of formal training (workshops, courses) and informal learning (mentorship, on-the-job training).
   - Decide whether training will be conducted in-house or outsourced to external trainers. Both options have their advantages depending on the expertise required.

4. **Choose Appropriate Training Methods:**
   - Select training methods that suit the content and learning preferences of your team. Common methods include:
     - **Workshops and Seminars:** Interactive sessions led by experts to teach specific skills or knowledge.
     - **Online Courses:** Flexible, self-paced learning through platforms like Coursera, Udemy, or LinkedIn Learning.
     - **On-the-Job Training:** Hands-on experience under the guidance of experienced colleagues.
     - **Mentorship Programs:** Pairing employees with mentors for personalized guidance and support.
     - **Role-Playing and Simulations:** Practical exercises that mimic real-world scenarios to enhance

problem-solving and decision-making skills.

5. **Implement the Training Program:**
    - Roll out the training program according to your plan. Ensure that all participants are informed about the schedule, objectives, and expectations.
    - Encourage active participation and create a supportive learning environment. Provide necessary resources and materials for effective learning.

6. **Evaluate and Adjust:**
    - Assess the effectiveness of your training program through feedback, quizzes, assessments, and performance metrics. Determine whether the training objectives were met and identify areas for improvement.
    - Use this feedback to refine and enhance future training sessions. Continuous evaluation ensures that your training program remains relevant and impactful.

Promoting Continuous Development

Training shouldn't be a one-time event but an ongoing process. Encourage continuous development through various initiatives:

1. **Create a Learning Culture:**
    - Foster a culture that values and prioritizes learning. Encourage employees to seek out learning opportunities and support their efforts to improve their skills.

- Celebrate learning achievements and recognize employees who take the initiative to develop their capabilities.

2. **Provide Access to Learning Resources:**
   - Offer access to online learning platforms, industry publications, and professional development resources. Create a library of materials that employees can use to enhance their knowledge.
   - Consider providing stipends or reimbursement for external courses, certifications, and conferences.

3. **Encourage Knowledge Sharing:**
   - Promote knowledge sharing within your team. Organize regular knowledge-sharing sessions where employees can present what they've learned to their colleagues.
   - Create a mentorship program where experienced employees can guide and support less experienced team members.

4. **Set Individual Development Plans (IDPs):**
   - Work with each employee to create an Individual Development Plan that outlines their career goals and the steps needed to achieve them. Regularly review and update these plans to ensure progress and alignment with business objectives.
   - IDPs help employees take ownership of their development and provide a clear roadmap for their growth within the company.

Real-Life Example:

Consider Alex, who manages a small software development company. Alex noticed that while his team was technically proficient, they lacked strong project management and communication skills. He conducted a training needs assessment and identified these areas as priorities.

Alex developed a training plan that included workshops on project management methodologies, online courses on effective communication, and a mentorship program pairing junior developers with senior team members. He also implemented role-playing exercises to improve problem-solving skills.

To promote continuous development, Alex provided access to online learning platforms and encouraged employees to attend industry conferences. He also established regular knowledge-sharing sessions where team members could present new techniques and best practices.

The result was a more skilled and cohesive team that managed projects more efficiently and communicated effectively with clients. The investment in training and development paid off through improved performance, higher employee satisfaction, and increased client satisfaction.

Conclusion

Training and development are vital for building a high-performing team. By assessing training needs, setting clear objectives, developing a comprehensive training plan, choosing appropriate methods, implementing the program, and promoting continuous learning, you can enhance your team's skills and keep them motivated. Investing in your employees' growth not only benefits them but also drives your business towards greater success. A well-trained and continuously developing team is the backbone of a thriving business.

Chapter 5

5. Scaling and Expansion

Scaling and expanding your small business can be one of the most exciting and rewarding phases of your entrepreneurial journey. This chapter will guide you through the essential strategies and considerations for successfully growing your business. Whether you're looking to increase your market presence, introduce new products or services, or enter new markets, careful planning and execution are crucial to sustainable growth.

Imagine your business as a growing tree. Just as a tree needs strong roots, adequate nutrients, and the right environment to thrive, your business requires a solid foundation, resources, and strategic planning to scale effectively. Scaling is not just about increasing sales or opening new locations; it's about ensuring that your business can handle growth without compromising on quality or customer satisfaction.

In this chapter, we will explore the key elements of scaling your business, including preparing for growth, scaling operations, leveraging technology, and entering new markets. We will also discuss the challenges you might face during this process and how to overcome them. Real-life examples and actionable insights will provide you with a roadmap to navigate the complexities of business expansion.

By the end of this chapter, you will have a comprehensive understanding of the steps required to scale your business successfully. You will be equipped with the knowledge to make informed decisions, manage risks, and capitalize on opportunities that come with growth. Let's embark on this journey of expansion and take your business to new heights.

5.1. Preparing for Growth

5.1.1. Scaling Operations

Scaling operations is a critical component of business growth. It involves expanding your production capacity, optimizing processes, and ensuring that your business can handle increased demand without compromising quality or efficiency. Here's how to effectively scale your operations to support business expansion.

1. Assess Your Current Operations

Before scaling, it's essential to have a thorough understanding of your current operations. Identify the strengths and weaknesses in your processes, resources, and capabilities.

- **Process Evaluation:** Map out your existing processes to pinpoint inefficiencies or bottlenecks. For example, if you run a manufacturing business, assess the workflow from raw material acquisition to finished product delivery.
- **Resource Analysis:** Evaluate your current resources, including staff, equipment, and technology. Determine if they can handle increased demand or if additional investments are necessary.

2. Develop a Scalable Business Model

A scalable business model is one that can grow without being hindered by its structure or resources. This involves creating systems and processes that can be easily expanded or replicated.

- **Standardize Processes:** Document your procedures and establish standard operating procedures (SOPs) that ensure consistency and efficiency. For example, a restaurant chain might standardize its recipes and kitchen processes to maintain quality across locations.
- **Automate Where Possible:** Leverage technology to automate repetitive tasks and streamline operations. Automation can reduce errors, save time, and free up staff to focus on more strategic activities.

3. Invest in Technology and Infrastructure

Investing in the right technology and infrastructure is crucial for scaling operations. Technology can enhance productivity, improve communication, and support data-driven decision-making.

- **Upgrade Systems:** Implement advanced software and tools that support your business needs. For instance, a robust enterprise resource planning (ERP) system can integrate various functions like inventory management, accounting, and customer relationship management (CRM).
- **Enhance IT Infrastructure:** Ensure that your IT infrastructure can handle increased activity. This might involve upgrading servers, improving

cybersecurity measures, or expanding your network capabilities.

4. Optimize Supply Chain Management

An efficient supply chain is vital for scaling operations. Ensure that your supply chain can accommodate increased production and distribution needs.

- **Strengthen Supplier Relationships:** Work closely with your suppliers to ensure they can meet your growing demands. Establish clear communication channels and negotiate favorable terms to support your expansion.
- **Inventory Management:** Implement inventory management practices that optimize stock levels and reduce carrying costs. Just-in-time (JIT) inventory systems can help maintain the right balance between supply and demand.

5. Build a Strong Team

A skilled and motivated team is essential for scaling operations. Invest in recruiting, training, and retaining employees who can support your growth objectives.

- **Hire Strategically:** Focus on hiring individuals with the skills and experience needed for your expanded operations. Look for team members who are adaptable and can thrive in a growing environment.
- **Training and Development:** Provide continuous training and development opportunities to equip your team with the necessary skills. This ensures that your staff can handle new responsibilities and contribute to the business's success.

6. Maintain Quality Control

As you scale, maintaining the quality of your products or services is crucial. Implement quality control measures to ensure consistency and meet customer expectations.

- **Quality Standards:** Establish clear quality standards and regularly monitor compliance. Use tools like checklists, audits, and feedback systems to maintain high standards.
- **Continuous Improvement:** Foster a culture of continuous improvement where employees are encouraged to identify areas for enhancement. Implementing small, incremental changes can lead to significant improvements over time.

7. Plan for Scalability in Marketing and Sales

Your marketing and sales efforts should also scale to support business growth. Develop strategies to reach a larger audience and convert leads into customers.

- **Expand Marketing Channels:** Use a mix of digital and traditional marketing channels to increase your reach. Invest in content marketing, social media, email campaigns, and search engine optimization (SEO) to attract new customers.
- **Sales Strategies:** Train your sales team to handle increased leads and close deals efficiently. Implement CRM systems to manage customer relationships and track sales performance.

Real-Life Example:

Consider the case of a successful online retailer looking to scale operations. Initially, the company faced challenges with manual order processing, limited warehouse space, and inconsistent product quality. To scale effectively, the retailer took several steps:

1. **Automated Order Processing:** The company implemented an e-commerce platform that automated order processing and inventory management, reducing errors and speeding up fulfillment.
2. **Expanded Warehouse Facilities:** They invested in larger warehouse spaces and optimized the layout for efficient storage and retrieval.
3. **Enhanced Quality Control:** The retailer established strict quality control protocols and regular audits to ensure product consistency.
4. **Technology Investment:** Upgraded their IT infrastructure to support higher traffic volumes and integrated systems for seamless operations.
5. **Marketing Expansion:** Launched comprehensive digital marketing campaigns and expanded their presence on various social media platforms.

As a result, the retailer successfully scaled its operations, improved customer satisfaction, and increased revenue.

Conclusion

Scaling operations is a complex but essential part of business growth. By assessing your current operations, developing a scalable business model, investing in technology and infrastructure, optimizing supply chain management, building a strong team, maintaining quality control, and planning for scalable marketing and sales, you can ensure that your business is well-prepared for expansion. These strategies will help you manage increased demand, maintain efficiency, and continue delivering high-quality products or services to your customers.

5.1.2. Leveraging Technology

Leveraging technology is crucial for scaling your small business. The right technological tools and systems can streamline operations, enhance productivity, and support your growth ambitions. By adopting advanced technologies, you can improve efficiency, reduce costs, and stay competitive in a rapidly evolving marketplace. Here's how to effectively leverage technology to support your business expansion.

1. Implement Robust Enterprise Resource Planning (ERP) Systems

An ERP system integrates various business functions into a single unified system, providing real-time visibility into your operations. It helps streamline processes, improve data accuracy, and enhance decision-making.

- **Benefits of ERP:** ERP systems consolidate data from different departments, such as finance, inventory, human resources, and sales, into one platform. This integration reduces data silos, improves communication, and enables efficient resource management.
- **Choosing an ERP System:** Select an ERP system that fits your business size and industry. Consider factors such as scalability, ease of use, customization options, and support services.

Popular ERP solutions for small businesses include SAP Business One, Oracle NetSuite, and Microsoft Dynamics 365.

2. Utilize Customer Relationship Management (CRM) Software

CRM software helps manage customer interactions, improve customer service, and drive sales growth. It provides valuable insights into customer behavior and preferences, enabling you to tailor your marketing and sales strategies.

- **Benefits of CRM:** CRM systems centralize customer data, track interactions, and automate tasks like follow-ups and marketing campaigns. This leads to improved customer retention, increased sales, and enhanced customer satisfaction.
- **Choosing a CRM System:** Consider features like contact management, sales automation, marketing tools, and analytics when selecting a CRM. Popular CRM solutions include Salesforce, HubSpot, and Zoho CRM.

3. Automate Routine Tasks

Automation can significantly enhance efficiency by reducing the time and effort spent on routine tasks. It allows your team to focus on more strategic activities, driving productivity and growth.

- **Areas for Automation:** Identify repetitive tasks that can be automated, such as data entry, invoice processing, email marketing, and customer support.

Automation tools like Zapier, UiPath, and Mailchimp can help streamline these processes.
- **Benefits of Automation:** Automation reduces human error, speeds up processes, and frees up resources for higher-value tasks. It also ensures consistency and reliability in operations.

4. Invest in E-commerce and Digital Platforms

For businesses looking to expand their market reach, investing in e-commerce and digital platforms is essential. These platforms enable you to sell products or services online, reaching a global audience.

- **Building an E-commerce Website:** Develop a user-friendly and mobile-responsive e-commerce website. Use platforms like Shopify, WooCommerce, or BigCommerce to create and manage your online store.
- **Leveraging Digital Marketplaces:** Consider selling on popular digital marketplaces like Amazon, eBay, and Etsy to increase visibility and sales. These platforms provide access to a large customer base and offer tools for managing listings, orders, and payments.

5. Enhance Cybersecurity Measures

As your business grows and adopts more technology, cybersecurity becomes increasingly important. Protecting your data and systems from cyber threats is crucial for maintaining business continuity and trust.

- **Implement Security Protocols:** Use firewalls, antivirus software, and encryption to safeguard

your data. Regularly update your systems and software to protect against vulnerabilities.
- **Employee Training:** Educate your employees about cybersecurity best practices, such as recognizing phishing attempts, using strong passwords, and securing their devices. Conduct regular training sessions to keep them informed about new threats and prevention methods.

6. Use Data Analytics for Informed Decision-Making

Data analytics provides valuable insights into your business performance and customer behavior. Leveraging data can help you make informed decisions, identify opportunities, and optimize operations.

- **Benefits of Data Analytics:** Analyzing data helps you understand trends, measure the effectiveness of marketing campaigns, forecast demand, and improve customer experiences.
- **Choosing Analytics Tools:** Select tools that offer comprehensive analytics capabilities, such as Google Analytics, Tableau, and Power BI. These tools can help you visualize data, generate reports, and gain actionable insights.

7. Embrace Cloud Computing

Cloud computing offers scalable and flexible solutions for data storage, collaboration, and application hosting. It allows you to access resources and services on-demand, supporting your growth needs.

- **Benefits of Cloud Computing:** Cloud solutions reduce the need for on-premises infrastructure,

lower IT costs, and enable remote work and collaboration. They also offer scalability, allowing you to adjust resources based on your business needs.
- **Choosing Cloud Providers:** Consider reputable cloud service providers like Amazon Web Services (AWS), Microsoft Azure, and Google Cloud. Evaluate their services, pricing, and support options to find the best fit for your business.

Real-Life Example:

Consider a small retail business looking to scale its operations. The owner decides to leverage technology to support this growth. They implement an ERP system to integrate inventory, sales, and finance functions, providing real-time visibility into their operations. They also adopt a CRM system to manage customer interactions and improve sales efficiency.

To enhance efficiency, the business automates routine tasks like order processing and email marketing. They invest in an e-commerce platform to reach a broader audience and increase sales. Recognizing the importance of cybersecurity, they implement robust security measures and train their employees on best practices.

By leveraging data analytics, the business gains insights into customer behavior and market trends, helping them make informed decisions. They also embrace cloud computing to enable remote work and scalable storage solutions. These technological advancements support the business's growth, improve efficiency, and enhance customer satisfaction.

Conclusion

Leveraging technology is essential for scaling your small business. By implementing robust ERP and CRM systems, automating routine tasks, investing in e-commerce and digital platforms, enhancing cybersecurity measures, using data analytics, and embracing cloud computing, you can streamline operations, improve efficiency, and support sustainable growth. These technological strategies will help you stay competitive, meet increased demand, and drive your business towards success.

5.2. Entering New Markets

5.2.1. Market Entry Strategies

Entering new markets is a significant step in expanding your small business. It opens up opportunities for growth, diversification, and increased revenue. However, successful market entry requires careful planning, research, and strategic execution. Here's how to develop and implement effective market entry strategies to ensure a smooth transition into new territories.

1. Conduct Thorough Market Research

Understanding the new market is crucial for successful entry. Comprehensive research helps you identify opportunities, assess risks, and tailor your approach to the local context.

- **Market Analysis:** Study the market size, growth potential, and competitive landscape. Identify key trends, customer preferences, and potential

barriers to entry. Use market reports, industry publications, and online resources to gather data.
- **Customer Insights:** Conduct surveys, focus groups, and interviews to understand the needs and preferences of your target audience in the new market. Analyze their buying behavior, pain points, and expectations.
- **Competitive Analysis:** Identify existing competitors and analyze their strengths, weaknesses, market share, and strategies. This helps you find gaps and opportunities to differentiate your business.

2. Choose the Right Market Entry Strategy

Selecting the appropriate market entry strategy depends on your business goals, resources, and the market environment. Common strategies include:

- **Exporting:** Selling your products or services directly to customers in the new market through online platforms or local distributors. This is a low-risk, cost-effective way to test the market.
- **Licensing and Franchising:** Allowing a local business to produce, market, and sell your products or services in exchange for royalties or fees. This strategy leverages local expertise and resources.
- **Joint Ventures and Partnerships:** Collaborating with a local partner to share resources, knowledge, and risks. Joint ventures provide access to local networks and expertise while sharing the investment and profits.
- **Direct Investment:** Establishing your own operations in the new market by setting up

subsidiaries, branches, or manufacturing facilities. This requires significant investment but offers greater control and potential for higher returns.
- **Mergers and Acquisitions:** Acquiring or merging with a local business to quickly gain market access, customer base, and local knowledge. This strategy can be complex and requires thorough due diligence.

3. Develop a Market Entry Plan

A well-structured market entry plan outlines your strategy, objectives, and the steps required to enter and succeed in the new market.

- **Objectives and Goals:** Define clear, measurable objectives for your market entry, such as revenue targets, market share, and customer acquisition goals. Align these with your overall business strategy.
- **Marketing and Sales Strategy:** Develop a tailored marketing and sales approach for the new market. Consider localization of your messaging, branding, and promotional activities to resonate with the local audience. Choose appropriate marketing channels, such as social media, local advertising, and events.
- **Pricing Strategy:** Determine a competitive pricing strategy that considers local purchasing power, competitor pricing, and your cost structure. Adapt your pricing model to the local market conditions.
- **Distribution and Logistics:** Plan your distribution channels and logistics to ensure efficient delivery of your products or services. Consider partnerships

with local distributors, third-party logistics providers, or setting up your own distribution network.

4. Build a Local Presence

Establishing a local presence helps build credibility, trust, and brand recognition in the new market.

- **Local Office or Store:** Setting up a local office or store can enhance your visibility and accessibility. It provides a physical location for customer interactions and support.
- **Hiring Local Talent:** Recruit local employees who understand the market, culture, and language. Local talent can provide valuable insights, foster relationships with local stakeholders, and improve customer engagement.
- **Networking and Partnerships:** Build relationships with local businesses, industry associations, and community organizations. Networking can open doors to new opportunities, collaborations, and market insights.

5. Monitor and Adapt

Entering a new market is an ongoing process that requires continuous monitoring and adaptation. Stay agile and responsive to changes in the market environment.

- **Performance Tracking:** Regularly monitor key performance indicators (KPIs) to assess your progress and identify areas for improvement. Use metrics such as sales, market share, customer feedback, and ROI.

- **Feedback Loop:** Collect feedback from customers, employees, and partners to understand their experiences and perspectives. Use this feedback to refine your strategies and address any issues.
- **Adaptation:** Be prepared to adjust your approach based on market dynamics, competition, and customer preferences. Flexibility and adaptability are key to long-term success in a new market.

Real-Life Example:

Consider a small organic skincare company looking to enter the European market. After conducting thorough market research, the company identified strong demand for natural skincare products and decided to start with exporting through online platforms and local distributors.

They developed a market entry plan that included localized marketing campaigns, competitive pricing strategies, and partnerships with eco-friendly retailers. To build a local presence, they hired a small team in Europe and participated in local beauty and wellness events to increase brand visibility.

By continuously monitoring their performance and adapting their strategies based on customer feedback and market trends, the company successfully established itself in the European market, achieving significant growth and brand recognition.

Conclusion

Entering new markets presents exciting opportunities for growth and expansion. By conducting thorough market research, choosing the right market entry strategy, developing a comprehensive plan, building a local presence, and continuously monitoring and adapting, you can successfully navigate the complexities of market entry. These strategies will help you capitalize on new opportunities, mitigate risks, and achieve sustainable growth in new territories.

5.2.2. INTERNATIONAL EXPANSION

Expanding your business internationally opens up a world of opportunities. It allows you to tap into new customer bases, diversify your revenue streams, and increase your brand's global presence. However, international expansion also comes with its own set of challenges and complexities. Here's how to navigate the process of entering international markets successfully.

1. Conduct In-Depth Market Research

Understanding the international market is crucial for success. Comprehensive research helps you identify opportunities, assess risks, and develop a tailored approach.

- **Market Analysis:** Study the market size, growth potential, and competitive landscape in the target country. Identify key trends, customer preferences, and potential barriers to entry. Use market reports, industry publications, and local experts to gather data.
- **Cultural Insights:** Understand the cultural nuances and consumer behavior in the target market. This includes preferences, values, and purchasing habits. Cultural insights help you tailor your products, marketing strategies, and customer interactions.

- **Regulatory Environment:** Research the regulatory requirements for doing business in the target country. This includes understanding trade laws, tariffs, import/export regulations, and local business laws. Compliance is critical to avoid legal issues and penalties.

2. Choose the Right Market Entry Strategy

Selecting the appropriate entry strategy depends on your business goals, resources, and the specific market conditions. Common strategies include:

- **Exporting:** Selling your products or services directly to customers in the international market. This can be done through online platforms, local distributors, or sales agents. Exporting is a low-risk way to test the market.
- **Licensing and Franchising:** Allowing a local business to use your brand, products, or services in exchange for royalties or fees. This strategy leverages local expertise and resources.
- **Joint Ventures and Partnerships:** Collaborating with a local partner to share resources, knowledge, and risks. Joint ventures provide access to local networks and expertise while sharing the investment and profits.
- **Foreign Direct Investment (FDI):** Establishing your own operations in the target country by setting up subsidiaries, branches, or manufacturing facilities. This requires significant investment but offers greater control and potential for higher returns.

- **Acquisitions:** Acquiring a local company to quickly gain market access, customer base, and local knowledge. This strategy can be complex and requires thorough due diligence.

3. Develop a Comprehensive International Expansion Plan

A well-structured plan outlines your strategy, objectives, and the steps required to enter and succeed in the international market.

- **Objectives and Goals:** Define clear, measurable objectives for your international expansion, such as revenue targets, market share, and customer acquisition goals. Align these with your overall business strategy.
- **Marketing and Sales Strategy:** Develop a tailored marketing and sales approach for the international market. Consider localization of your messaging, branding, and promotional activities to resonate with the local audience. Choose appropriate marketing channels, such as social media, local advertising, and events.
- **Pricing Strategy:** Determine a competitive pricing strategy that considers local purchasing power, competitor pricing, and your cost structure. Adapt your pricing model to the local market conditions.
- **Distribution and Logistics:** Plan your distribution channels and logistics to ensure efficient delivery of your products or services. Consider partnerships with local distributors, third-party logistics providers, or setting up your own distribution network.

4. Build a Local Presence

Establishing a local presence helps build credibility, trust, and brand recognition in the international market.

- **Local Office or Store:** Setting up a local office or store can enhance your visibility and accessibility. It provides a physical location for customer interactions and support.
- **Hiring Local Talent:** Recruit local employees who understand the market, culture, and language. Local talent can provide valuable insights, foster relationships with local stakeholders, and improve customer engagement.
- **Networking and Partnerships:** Build relationships with local businesses, industry associations, and community organizations. Networking can open doors to new opportunities, collaborations, and market insights.

5. Monitor and Adapt

Entering an international market is an ongoing process that requires continuous monitoring and adaptation. Stay agile and responsive to changes in the market environment.

- **Performance Tracking:** Regularly monitor key performance indicators (KPIs) to assess your progress and identify areas for improvement. Use metrics such as sales, market share, customer feedback, and ROI.
- **Feedback Loop:** Collect feedback from customers, employees, and partners to understand their experiences and perspectives. Use this feedback to refine your strategies and address any issues.

- **Adaptation:** Be prepared to adjust your approach based on market dynamics, competition, and customer preferences. Flexibility and adaptability are key to long-term success in an international market.

Real-Life Example:

Consider a small U.S.-based organic skincare company looking to expand into the European market. After conducting thorough market research, the company identified strong demand for natural skincare products in Europe and decided to start with exporting through online platforms and local distributors.

They developed a comprehensive international expansion plan that included localized marketing campaigns, competitive pricing strategies, and partnerships with eco-friendly retailers. To build a local presence, they hired a small team in Europe and participated in local beauty and wellness events to increase brand visibility.

By continuously monitoring their performance and adapting their strategies based on customer feedback and market trends, the company successfully established itself in the European market, achieving significant growth and brand recognition.

Conclusion

International expansion presents exciting opportunities for growth and diversification. By conducting thorough market research, choosing the right market entry strategy, developing a comprehensive plan, building a local presence, and continuously monitoring and adapting, you can successfully navigate the complexities of entering international markets. These strategies will help you capitalize on new opportunities, mitigate risks, and achieve sustainable growth on a global scale.

Conclusion

As we draw this journey to a close, it's important to reflect on the incredible path you've embarked upon in mastering small business success. The strategies and insights shared throughout this book are designed to equip you with the knowledge and tools needed to build, grow, and sustain a thriving business. From the foundational elements of market research and branding to the advanced tactics of scaling and international expansion, each chapter has been crafted to provide practical, actionable advice tailored to the unique challenges and opportunities faced by small business owners.

Imagine your business as a seed that has been carefully nurtured through each stage of its growth. You've learned how to plant it in fertile soil by understanding your market and defining your vision. You've watered it consistently with effective marketing strategies and financial management techniques. You've provided it with the necessary nutrients through strong leadership and team-building practices. And as it begins to flourish, you've expanded its reach with thoughtful scaling and market entry strategies.

The journey of a small business owner is filled with both triumphs and trials. There will be moments of exhilarating success and inevitable setbacks. However, with the right mindset and a solid plan, you are well-equipped to navigate the challenges and seize the opportunities that come your way. Remember, the key to lasting success lies in your ability to adapt, innovate, and remain resilient.

As you continue on this path, let the lessons and examples shared in this book serve as your guide and inspiration. Your dedication, hard work, and passion are the driving forces behind your business's success. Embrace the journey with confidence and courage, knowing that you have the knowledge and tools to achieve your goals and make a lasting impact.

REFLECTING ON THE JOURNEY

KEY TAKEAWAYS

Reflecting on the journey of building and growing your small business provides an opportunity to consolidate the key takeaways from your experiences. These insights serve as a foundation for future success and continuous improvement. Let's revisit the essential lessons and strategies covered in this book, highlighting their importance and application.

1. The Backbone of the Economy

Small businesses are the backbone of the economy, driving innovation, creating jobs, and contributing to the community. Understanding this role emphasizes the significance of your efforts and the impact you can have. Always remember that your business, regardless of its size, plays a vital part in the larger economic landscape.

2. Vision and Mission

Defining a clear vision and mission is crucial for setting the direction of your business. Your vision outlines your long-term aspirations, while your mission defines the purpose and core values that guide your daily operations. Together, they provide a roadmap for decision-making and strategic planning.

3. Market Research and Target Audience

Understanding your market and identifying your target audience are foundational steps in building a successful business. Conduct thorough market research to gather insights into industry trends, customer needs, and competitive dynamics. Knowing your target audience helps tailor your products, services, and marketing efforts to meet their specific needs and preferences.

4. Branding and Positioning

A strong brand identity and effective positioning differentiate your business from competitors and create a lasting impression on customers. Develop a compelling brand story, consistent visual identity, and clear messaging. Position your brand strategically in the market to highlight your unique value proposition.

5. Marketing Strategies

Effective marketing strategies are essential for attracting and retaining customers. Utilize a mix of digital and traditional marketing techniques to reach your target audience. Focus on creating engaging content, leveraging social media, optimizing for search engines, and building strong customer relationships through personalized communication.

6. Financial Management

Sound financial management is critical for the sustainability and growth of your business. Create realistic budgets, forecast financial performance, and manage cash flow effectively. Regularly review financial statements to monitor your business's health and make informed decisions. Invest in accounting software and seek professional advice when needed.

7. Leadership and Team Building

Effective leadership and team building are key to fostering a positive work environment and achieving business goals. Lead by example, motivate your team, and invest in their professional development. Building a high-performing team requires recruiting the right talent, providing continuous training, and fostering a culture of collaboration and accountability.

8. Scaling and Expansion

Scaling your business involves expanding operations, optimizing processes, and leveraging technology to handle increased demand. Prepare for growth by assessing your current capabilities, developing a scalable business model, and investing in the right infrastructure. Entering new markets requires thorough research, strategic planning, and a tailored approach to local conditions.

9. Overcoming Challenges

Every business faces challenges, from financial setbacks to competitive pressures. The ability to overcome these obstacles lies in your resilience and adaptability. Embrace a problem-solving mindset, seek support from mentors and networks, and continuously learn from your experiences. Turn challenges into opportunities for growth and improvement.

10. Continuous Improvement

Continuous improvement is the hallmark of a successful business. Regularly evaluate your strategies, processes, and performance. Solicit feedback from customers, employees, and stakeholders to identify areas for enhancement. Stay abreast of industry trends and innovations to remain competitive and relevant.

Real-Life Application:

Consider Jane, who runs a boutique marketing agency. By applying the lessons from this book, Jane has successfully navigated the complexities of growing her business. She started with a clear vision and mission, which guided her strategic decisions. Through diligent market research, she identified her niche and tailored her services to meet the needs of small businesses in her area.

Jane developed a strong brand identity that resonated with her target audience. Her marketing strategies, a blend of digital and traditional methods, effectively attracted and retained clients. By maintaining sound financial practices, Jane ensured her agency's sustainability and growth.

Her leadership skills fostered a motivated and high-performing team. Jane's investment in training and development created a culture of continuous learning and improvement. As her business grew, she scaled operations by adopting new technologies and entering new markets with a well-researched strategy.

Jane faced challenges along the way, but her resilience and adaptability turned obstacles into stepping stones. Regular evaluations and feedback loops helped her refine her strategies and stay ahead of the competition. Jane's journey exemplifies the application of the key takeaways from this book.

Conclusion

Reflecting on your journey and the key takeaways from this book empowers you to apply these lessons to your business. Embrace your role in the economy, define a clear vision and mission, understand your market, build a strong brand, implement effective marketing strategies, manage finances wisely, lead and build your team, scale and expand strategically, overcome challenges, and commit to continuous improvement. These principles are the foundation of your business success. As you move forward, let these insights guide your decisions and actions, ensuring sustained growth and lasting impact.

Future Outlook

As you look towards the future of your small business, it's important to envision the path ahead with a blend of optimism and strategic planning. The landscape of entrepreneurship is continually evolving, influenced by technological advancements, market trends, and societal shifts. Embracing this dynamic environment with a forward-thinking mindset will help you navigate the challenges and seize the opportunities that lie ahead. Let's explore key considerations for shaping a promising future for your business.

1. Embrace Innovation and Technology

Technology is a driving force in today's business world, offering tools and solutions that can transform how you operate and compete. Embrace innovation to stay ahead of the curve.

- **Adopt Emerging Technologies:** Keep an eye on emerging technologies that can enhance your business operations, such as artificial intelligence, blockchain, and the Internet of Things (IoT). These technologies can improve efficiency, security, and customer experience.
- **Invest in Digital Transformation:** Digital transformation involves integrating digital technologies into all areas of your business, fundamentally changing how you deliver value to customers. This includes automating processes, leveraging data analytics, and enhancing online presence.

2. Focus on Sustainability and Social Responsibility

Sustainability and social responsibility are increasingly important to consumers, investors, and stakeholders. Incorporating these principles into your business can drive long-term success and positive impact.

- **Sustainable Practices:** Implement sustainable practices in your operations, such as reducing waste, conserving energy, and sourcing eco-friendly

materials. This not only benefits the environment but also appeals to eco-conscious consumers.
- **Corporate Social Responsibility (CSR):** Develop CSR initiatives that align with your values and mission. This could involve community engagement, charitable contributions, and ethical business practices. Demonstrating a commitment to social responsibility can enhance your brand reputation and customer loyalty.

3. Cultivate Agility and Adaptability

The ability to adapt quickly to changing circumstances is a key determinant of business success. Cultivate a culture of agility and adaptability within your organization.

- **Responsive Planning:** Implement responsive planning processes that allow you to pivot quickly when necessary. This includes scenario planning, real-time data analysis, and flexible strategies.
- **Employee Empowerment:** Empower your employees to make decisions and take initiative. A culture of adaptability requires a team that is proactive, innovative, and willing to embrace change.

4. Strengthen Customer Relationships

Strong customer relationships are the foundation of a successful business. Focus on building and maintaining these relationships to ensure customer loyalty and satisfaction.

- **Personalized Experiences:** Use data and customer insights to create personalized experiences that

meet individual needs and preferences. This could involve customized product recommendations, tailored marketing messages, and personalized customer service.
- **Continuous Engagement:** Maintain continuous engagement with your customers through various touchpoints, such as social media, email marketing, and loyalty programs. Regular communication helps build trust and keeps your brand top-of-mind.

5. Expand and Diversify

Growth often involves expanding your market reach and diversifying your offerings. Consider strategies for both horizontal and vertical growth.

- **New Markets:** Explore new geographic markets or customer segments to expand your reach. This could involve entering international markets or targeting underserved demographics.
- **Product Diversification:** Introduce new products or services that complement your existing offerings. Diversification can reduce risk and open up new revenue streams.

6. Invest in Talent Development

Your team is one of your most valuable assets. Investing in their development ensures that you have the skills and capabilities needed to drive future growth.

- **Continuous Learning:** Provide opportunities for continuous learning and professional development. This could include training programs, workshops, and access to online courses.

- **Leadership Development:** Develop future leaders within your organization by offering leadership training and mentorship programs. Strong leadership is crucial for navigating the complexities of business growth.

7. Monitor Industry Trends

Staying informed about industry trends helps you anticipate changes and position your business for success.

- **Market Research:** Conduct regular market research to identify emerging trends, customer preferences, and competitive dynamics. Use this information to inform your strategic decisions.
- **Industry Networking:** Participate in industry events, conferences, and professional associations. Networking with industry peers can provide valuable insights and opportunities for collaboration.

Real-Life Example:

Consider a small tech startup that began by developing software solutions for local businesses. By embracing innovation, the startup adopted cloud computing and AI to enhance their product offerings. They also implemented sustainable practices, such as energy-efficient servers and paperless operations, appealing to eco-conscious clients.

The startup cultivated a culture of agility by empowering employees to innovate and respond quickly to market changes. They strengthened customer relationships through personalized service and regular engagement. As they grew, they expanded into international markets and diversified their product line to include mobile apps and cybersecurity solutions.

Investing in talent development, the startup provided continuous learning opportunities and leadership training for their team. By staying informed about industry trends and maintaining a flexible approach, they successfully navigated the challenges of growth and established themselves as a leader in their field.

Conclusion

The future of your small business holds immense potential. By embracing innovation, focusing on sustainability, cultivating agility, strengthening customer relationships, expanding and diversifying, investing in talent development, and monitoring industry trends, you can position your business for sustained success. As you move forward, let these principles guide your actions and decisions, ensuring that your business remains resilient, competitive, and impactful in the years to come.

FINAL THOUGHTS AND ENCOURAGEMENT

STAYING RESILIENT

Resilience is a crucial trait for any entrepreneur. The journey of running a small business is filled with ups and downs, challenges, and unexpected obstacles. Staying resilient means being able to bounce back from setbacks, adapt to changing circumstances, and maintain a positive outlook even in tough times. In this section, we will explore the importance of resilience and how to cultivate it to ensure the long-term success of your business.

1. Embrace a Growth Mindset

A growth mindset is the belief that abilities and intelligence can be developed through dedication and hard work. This mindset fosters resilience by encouraging you to view challenges as opportunities for growth.

- **Learn from Failures:** Instead of fearing failure, view it as a learning experience. Analyze what went wrong, identify lessons learned, and apply them to future endeavors. This approach helps you grow stronger and more capable.
- **Celebrate Small Wins:** Recognize and celebrate your achievements, no matter how small. Celebrating progress boosts morale and reinforces your commitment to your goals.

2. Build a Support Network

A strong support network provides emotional and practical assistance during challenging times. Surround yourself with people who encourage and inspire you.

- **Mentorship:** Seek out mentors who can offer guidance, advice, and perspective based on their experiences. Mentors can provide valuable insights and help you navigate difficult situations.
- **Peer Support:** Connect with other entrepreneurs and business owners. Sharing experiences and challenges with peers can provide a sense of camaraderie and collective wisdom.

3. Maintain a Healthy Work-Life Balance

Balancing work and personal life is essential for sustaining long-term resilience. Overworking can lead to burnout, while a balanced approach ensures you remain energized and focused.

- **Set Boundaries:** Establish clear boundaries between work and personal life. Allocate specific times for work and stick to them, allowing yourself time to recharge.
- **Self-Care:** Prioritize self-care activities such as exercise, meditation, hobbies, and spending time with loved ones. Taking care of your physical and mental well-being enhances your ability to cope with stress.

4. Stay Adaptable and Flexible

Adaptability is a key component of resilience. The ability to pivot and adjust your strategies in response to changing circumstances ensures your business remains viable.

- **Embrace Change:** View change as an opportunity rather than a threat. Stay open to new ideas, technologies, and approaches that can improve your business.
- **Plan for Contingencies:** Develop contingency plans for potential challenges. Having a backup plan in place provides a sense of security and readiness to handle unexpected events.

5. Focus on Your Vision and Purpose

A clear vision and sense of purpose provide direction and motivation, especially during tough times. Remind yourself why you started your business and the impact you want to achieve.

- **Reconnect with Your Mission:** Regularly revisit your business mission and values. This helps reinforce your commitment and provides a sense of meaning.
- **Inspire Your Team:** Share your vision with your team and inspire them to work towards common goals. A motivated and aligned team contributes to a resilient organization.

6. Practice Mindfulness and Stress Management

Mindfulness and stress management techniques help you stay grounded and calm in the face of adversity.

- **Mindfulness Practices:** Incorporate mindfulness practices such as meditation, deep breathing, or yoga into your daily routine. These practices help reduce stress and improve focus.
- **Stress Management:** Identify stress triggers and develop strategies to manage them effectively. This could include time management techniques, delegating tasks, or seeking professional support when needed.

7. Continuously Learn and Improve

Lifelong learning and continuous improvement are essential for staying resilient and competitive in the business world.

- **Stay Informed:** Keep up with industry trends, market developments, and emerging technologies.

Staying informed helps you anticipate changes and adapt proactively.
- **Invest in Skills Development:** Regularly invest in developing new skills and enhancing existing ones. This not only improves your capabilities but also boosts your confidence and resilience.

Real-Life Example:

Consider Maria, who runs a small bakery. During the economic downturn, Maria faced significant challenges, including reduced customer footfall and increased costs. Instead of giving up, Maria embraced a growth mindset. She analyzed the situation, sought advice from her mentor, and identified new opportunities.

Maria diversified her product offerings to include online orders and delivery services, adapting to the changing market conditions. She maintained a healthy work-life balance by setting clear boundaries and prioritizing self-care. Her strong support network, including fellow business owners and her family, provided encouragement and practical support.

By staying adaptable, focusing on her vision, and practicing mindfulness, Maria navigated the tough times and emerged stronger. Her bakery not only survived but thrived, thanks to her resilience and proactive approach.

Conclusion

Staying resilient is vital for long-term success in the entrepreneurial journey. Embrace a growth mindset, build a support network, maintain a healthy work-life balance, stay adaptable, focus on your vision, practice mindfulness, and commit to continuous learning. These strategies will help you navigate challenges, seize opportunities, and sustain your business over time. Remember, resilience is not about avoiding difficulties but about facing them with strength and determination. As you move forward, let resilience be your guiding force, empowering you to achieve your goals and make a lasting impact.

Continuous Improvement

Continuous improvement is the practice of consistently seeking ways to enhance your business processes, products, and services. It involves a commitment to ongoing learning, adaptation, and innovation. By fostering a culture of continuous improvement, you can stay competitive, meet evolving customer needs, and drive long-term success. Let's explore the importance of continuous improvement and how to embed it into your business operations.

1. Embrace a Culture of Learning

A culture of learning encourages everyone in your organization to seek knowledge and skill enhancement. This mindset is foundational to continuous improvement.

- **Encourage Curiosity:** Foster an environment where curiosity is valued. Encourage employees to ask questions, seek new knowledge, and explore innovative solutions.
- **Provide Learning Opportunities:** Offer access to training programs, workshops, webinars, and online courses. Support employees in pursuing further education and professional development.

2. Implement Feedback Loops

Regular feedback from customers, employees, and other stakeholders is crucial for identifying areas for improvement.

- **Customer Feedback:** Actively seek customer feedback through surveys, reviews, and direct interactions. Analyze this feedback to understand customer needs and expectations. Use it to make informed decisions about product and service enhancements.
- **Employee Feedback:** Create channels for employees to share their insights and suggestions. Regularly conduct employee surveys and hold feedback sessions. This not only identifies areas for improvement but also fosters a sense of ownership and engagement.

3. Utilize Data and Analytics

Data-driven decision-making is essential for effective continuous improvement. Leverage data and analytics to gain insights into your business performance.

- **Track Key Metrics:** Identify key performance indicators (KPIs) relevant to your business goals. Regularly monitor these metrics to assess progress and identify trends.
- **Analyze and Act:** Use data analytics tools to analyze performance data. Identify patterns, pinpoint inefficiencies, and make data-driven decisions to optimize processes and outcomes.

4. Adopt Lean Principles

Lean principles focus on maximizing value by minimizing waste. Implementing lean methodologies can streamline operations and improve efficiency.

- **Value Stream Mapping:** Map out your processes to identify value-adding and non-value-adding activities. Focus on eliminating waste and optimizing the flow of value to the customer.
- **Continuous Improvement Cycles:** Use continuous improvement cycles, such as Plan-Do-Check-Act (PDCA), to systematically address inefficiencies. Implement changes, monitor results, and make further adjustments as needed.

5. Foster Innovation

Innovation is a key driver of continuous improvement. Encourage creative thinking and experimentation within your organization.

- **Innovation Programs:** Establish programs that promote innovation, such as idea competitions, hackathons, and innovation labs. Provide resources and support for employees to develop and test new ideas.
- **Collaborative Innovation:** Foster collaboration across departments and teams. Encourage diverse perspectives and cross-functional teamwork to generate innovative solutions.

6. Benchmarking

Benchmarking involves comparing your business processes and performance metrics to industry best practices or competitors. This helps identify areas for improvement and set performance targets.

- **Internal Benchmarking:** Compare performance across different departments or units within your organization. Identify best practices and replicate them across the business.
- **External Benchmarking:** Study industry leaders and competitors to understand their strategies and performance levels. Use this information to set ambitious but achievable goals.

7. Commit to Sustainability

Sustainability practices not only benefit the environment but also drive long-term business improvement and resilience.

- **Sustainable Practices:** Implement environmentally friendly practices, such as reducing energy consumption, minimizing waste, and using sustainable materials. These practices can reduce costs and enhance your brand reputation.
- **Corporate Social Responsibility (CSR):** Develop CSR initiatives that align with your business values and mission. Engaging in community projects and ethical practices strengthens stakeholder relationships and supports continuous improvement.

Real-Life Example:

Consider a small manufacturing company that has embedded continuous improvement into its operations.

The company encourages a culture of learning by providing ongoing training and development programs for employees. It actively seeks customer and employee feedback to identify areas for improvement.

Using data analytics, the company tracks key metrics such as production efficiency, defect rates, and customer satisfaction. It adopts lean principles to streamline processes and reduce waste. Regular benchmarking against industry standards helps set performance targets and identify best practices.

To foster innovation, the company holds quarterly innovation workshops where employees can pitch ideas and work on creative projects. It also commits to sustainability by implementing energy-efficient processes and participating in community environmental initiatives.

These continuous improvement practices have led to significant gains in efficiency, product quality, and customer satisfaction. The company's proactive approach to improvement ensures it remains competitive and resilient in a dynamic market.

Conclusion

Continuous improvement is essential for sustaining long-term success in a competitive business environment. By embracing a culture of learning, implementing feedback loops, utilizing data and analytics, adopting lean principles, fostering innovation, benchmarking, and committing to sustainability, you can drive ongoing enhancements in your business. These practices will help you stay adaptable, meet evolving customer needs, and achieve sustained growth. Remember, the journey of improvement is never-ending. Continuously seek ways to refine your processes, products, and services to maintain your competitive edge and achieve lasting success.

A Personal Message and Acknowledgements

As we come to the end of this journey, I want to express my deepest gratitude to everyone who has supported me in the creation of this book. This project would not have been possible without the encouragement, insights, and expertise of many individuals.

First and foremost, I would like to thank my family for their unwavering support and understanding throughout this process. Their patience and encouragement have been invaluable.

A special thank you goes to my mentors and colleagues who provided guidance, shared their knowledge, and believed in the vision of this book. Your contributions have been instrumental in shaping the content and ensuring its practical relevance.

To my readers, thank you for taking the time to read this book. Your feedback is incredibly valuable to me. If you found the insights and strategies in this book helpful, I kindly invite you to leave a review. Your thoughts and experiences will help others on their entrepreneurial journey.

Nolan Davis

www.ingramcontent.com/pod-product-compliance
Lightning Source LLC
Chambersburg PA
CBHW052209220526
45471CB00004B/1886